ANGELS IN THE ARMY

ANGELS IN THE ARMY

HOW TO RELEASE THE HEAVENLY HOST IN SPIRITUAL WARFARE

DALE M. SIDES

The scripture used throughout this study is quoted from the King James Version unless otherwise noted. Bolded words within a verse indicate the author's emphasis and any explanatory words inserted by the author are enclosed in brackets [ ].

Angels in the Army
Copyright © 2004
Liberating Publications, Inc.
ISBN 1-930433-20-4

All rights reserved. No part of this book may be reproduced or transmitted in any form or by any means, electronic or mechanical, including photocopying, recording, or by any information storage and retrieval system, without permission in writing from the publisher.

"The War Rules" have been taken from *The Dead Sea Scrolls in English*, revised and extended fourth edition, Penguin Books Ltd., p.123-145. © 1962 by Geza Vermes. Used by permission. The excerpts that have been specifically referenced within *Angels in the Army* are underlined in the appendix.

Printed in Colombia

Table of Contents

Introduction ... 1

Chapter 1:
A Taxonomy of Angels ... 7

Chapter 2:
Angels AND Men in the Army ... 21

Chapter 3:
Order in the Army ... 27

Chapter 4:
Executing the Word of the Lord ... 37

Chapter 5:
If the Trumpet Makes an Uncertain Sound,
Who Will Prepare for Battle? ... 45

Conclusion:
Take Up Serpents and Subdue the Enemy ... 55

Notes ... 59

Appendix A: The War Rules ... 63

Appendix B: Let the Angel of the Lord
Chase Them ... 97

Scripture Index ... 103

> Bless the LORD, ye his angels,
> that excel in strength, that do
> his commandments, hearkening
> unto the voice of his word.
> Psalm 103:20

DEDICATION

> Dedicated to Harold Edward Sides,
> my father, example, mentor, coach, friend
> and fellow prayer-warrior, whose character
> and Christian witness will forever be
> the benchmark of virtue for my life.

> Bless ye the LORD, all ye
> his hosts; ye ministers of his,
> that do his pleasure.
> Psalm 103:21

INTRODUCTION

The subject of angels and their relationship with people has both fascinated and baffled mankind throughout history. We have run the gamut of responses to them—we have feared them, neglected them, worshipped them, given them wings and a halo, dressed them in fairy costumes, and given them a lyre or a cupid's bow. Replicas of angels guard mysterious dark castles and even the ancient Ark of the Covenant.

The imagination of mankind runs wild trying to describe these heavenly creatures. Over 80 percent of Americans polled[1] believe in their existence, and it is not uncommon to hear someone say that an "unexplainable creature" intervened in his or her life. Although the existence of angels is an accepted reality for many people, they usually cannot explain the reason for their existence.

The Bible makes it clear that angels of God are mighty warriors in the spirit realm. It records them marching through the tops of mulberry trees, defeating the armies of the Philistines, flattening the walls of

Jericho, annihilating the Assyrian army, and fighting to defeat the army of Sisera. We read of angels shutting the mouths of lions and opening the mouth of Balaam's ass.

There is no doubt about the existence of angels or their ability and power. Psalm 103:20 says that they excel in strength. But do we have the ability to contact these mighty warriors and, if so, what would be the purpose for interaction with them?

Warfare is going on in the heavenly realm and the key to winning this war is to know how to engage the angels, the mighty ones, in the spiritual battle. Jesus commissioned us, His earthly people, to do this and gave the church the keys and authority to marshal heavenly warfare by dispatching the angels of God into this spiritual campaign. He not only gave His disciples the orders to confront the enemy, but also to build the kingdom of heaven on this earth. This is done by the principle of binding and loosing—evil forces in the heavens are bound as we loose the angels into battle.

> *And I will give unto thee the keys of the kingdom of heaven: and whatsoever thou shalt bind on earth shall be bound in heaven: and whatsoever thou shalt loose on earth shall be loosed in heaven.*
> *Matthew 16:19*

Jesus said that by this principle the church would be built and the gates of hell would not prevail against it (verse 18). If we are to honestly evaluate our success we must ask ourselves: have the gates of hell prevailed against the church? Have we been as successful in waging war against God's enemies as we should have

Introduction

been? Are we in fact consistently winning the battle? It is time to get honest with ourselves and with the Lord.

Isn't it obvious that we have missed some fundamental key to understanding the rules of this warfare? We must consult our war manual, the Bible, to find the missing information in order to build God's kingdom through subduing the spirit realm. The pivotal responsibility we hold in engaging the heavenly realm can no longer be neglected.

> *To the intent that now unto the principalities and powers in heavenly places might be known **by the church** the manifold wisdom of God.*
> Ephesians 3:10

Jesus assigned the keys to building the kingdom of God on earth to us—His authorities and rulers upon the earth. Through the operation of binding and loosing, whatever we release in the heavenly realm will be unleashed upon the enemy by the hands of these mighty angelic warriors, and whatever we bind from the earth will be bound by our warring comrades.

In this book, we will go deep into the Bible and discuss the operation of this powerful key of binding and loosing angels into battle. Notice that before Jesus issued the Great Commission in Matthew 28:19 and 20 (to establish the kingdom of God on the earth), He gave us the keys to controlling the heavenly realm (Matthew 16:19). All warfare, both spiritual and physical, teaches us the same lessons we learned as kids playing King of the Mountain: if you want to win, you must take and control the high ground. In order to sustain a successful campaign on the earth, we must

Angels in the Army

first learn to control the heavenlies. The principle of controlling the heavens comes before waging war on the earth.

As brash as this may sound, I submit to you that there are basic principles of evangelism and kingdom building that we have missed. I heard a shocking statement recently that shows our lack of success in kingdom domination: even after 2,000 years, almost 40 percent of the world have never even heard the name of Jesus Christ, while 95 percent know the name of Coca-Cola. I believe that the early church lost the basic principles of Jesus' revelation on how to build the kingdom of God on the earth and, consequently, mankind suffered through the Dark Ages.

In my quest and zeal to understand the principles of spiritual warfare, I have pored over the Bible to seek out any missing ingredient. There may be other principles that we need to recover, but I guarantee you that I have found at least one, validated by the fact that it will be the first weapon Jesus will deploy when He returns to earth. He will operate the key of authority—binding and loosing. From the word that comes out of His mouth (Revelation 19:15), Jesus will loose an angel to bind Satan for a thousand years. He will finally culminate the domination over Satan, which He authorized us to enforce for the past 2,000 years.

> *And I saw an angel come down from heaven, having the key of the bottomless pit and a great chain in his hand. And he laid hold on the dragon, that old serpent, which is the Devil, and Satan, and **bound** him a thousand years.*
> *Revelation 20:1–2*

Introduction

In my first book on spiritual warfare, *God Damn Satan,* I promised that I would write a sequel entitled *Spiritual Warfare Strategies from the Dead Sea Scrolls.* This book is the fulfillment of that promise, but with a different title. Although it would greatly benefit your understanding to read *God Damn Satan* before reading *Angels In the Army,* it is not absolutely necessary. I believe this work can also stand alone because it provides practical instruction on how the church interacts with the angels of God, thus fulfilling our responsibility of releasing them into warfare in the heavenly realm.

The major point we have missed is *how* to engage the angels into spiritual battle. This strategy will be discussed throughout the body of the book and will be further clarified by a close scrutiny of Appendix A—The War Rules from the Dead Sea Scrolls.

When we dust off the manuscripts which were packed away in the Qumran caves about 150 B.C., we will realize that we have missed some vital principles. God had the scrolls recovered just in time to equip His army for the end-time march and conquest of the world. This is *big* medicine!

There are angels in the army of the Lord and there are people in the army of the Lord, too. We will discover the relationship between them, and the nature of their interaction. As disciples we must understand our function in our divinely commissioned rulership over the earth. We must take on this responsibility if we are to build the kingdom of God and we can begin this by studying and learning our role of binding and loosing to release the angels into battle. We have the means to close the gates of hell and release the blessings of heaven upon the earth.

Let's explore the massive power of these mighty warriors and the authority that we, the disciples of the Lord, have to release them into battle. Hordes of evil angels are cowering in fear that you will read and practice what is written here.

> *Behold, I give unto you power to tread on serpents and scorpions, and over all the power of the enemy: and nothing shall by any means hurt you.*
> *Luke 10:19*

> *The angel of the LORD encampeth round about them that fear him, and delivereth them.*
> *Psalm 34:7*

Angels are created beings and, as with all created things, they have a purpose in God's plan. They were created to serve, primarily to serve God, but also mankind. They serve as worshipers, warriors, messengers and workers, all under orders from legitimate authorities. Not realizing the complete spectrum of their purpose has caused us to misunderstand their function and our relationship with them.

Mankind was also created by God to fulfill His plan—to rule over God's creation (Genesis 1:28). Herein lies the focal point of our study—God has assigned angels to help us rule over His creation. Hallelujah!

CHAPTER 1
A TAXONOMY OF ANGELS

Many fine books have been written about angels, however this book will include a section of fundamental understanding that is often missing—our working relationship with them. God made mankind to rule over His creation and He assigned certain kinds of angels to assist us. Because we are focused on the working relationship that we as Christians have with angels and the specifics of interfacing with them, we need to set forth a clear-cut classification of these heavenly creatures. There are different categories of angels and each has specific functions. Ignorance of this has led to erroneous conclusions about our relationship with angels and unfortunate misunderstanding and misapplication of this entire subject.

Assigning taxonomy means to classify items (in this case angels) and to define the specific function of each category. For example, maples, oaks, and dogwoods are all trees, and the taxonomy of these three would be: *acer, quercus,* and *cornus.* "Angels" would be the overall classification (like "trees"), and their taxonomy will categorize and classify them according to function and location. When we understand the taxonomy of angels, we will see that they are not all the same; they actually have different functions and likewise produce different results.

When it comes to the subject of our relationship with angels, a commonly asked question is, "Do we have authority over angels, and can we actually command them into battle?" The accurate answer to this (although it sounds like a politician's answer) is, "Yes and no." As we begin to look at the taxonomy of angels we will understand this answer. We do have authority to command some angels, but we do not have authority to command all of them.

The word "angel" is a generic term we use to describe our heavenly allies.[2] It comes from the Greek word *aggelos*, which in it simplest form means "messenger."[3] The Hebrew equivalent is the word *malak*,[4] which also has the generic definition of messenger. "Angel" is a very generic term, and when we fully classify them and arrange the taxonomy, we will see that there are actually seven different kinds of angels.[5] This information will help clear up any potential confusion about our relationship with them and whether or not we have authority to direct angels in battle.

Before getting into the specifics of each category of angels, we need to recall that our purpose in doing so is not preoccupation and/or fascination with these heavenly beings.[6] *The reason for our study is to more effectively engage in spiritual warfare in partnership*

A Taxonomy of Angels

with these creatures who excel in strength.

Here is an overview of the taxonomy: God assigned four kinds of angels to minister primarily in heaven, and He assigned three kinds to minister primarily on earth. The ones assigned to heavenly functions are: cherubim, seraphim, living creatures, and worshipping spirits. Mankind has no jurisdiction over these four. The three assigned to function on earth are: watchers,[7] archangels, and ministering spirits. These do come under man's authority within the army of the Lord. For the benefit of our study and classification, we will discuss each category and then I will provide a synopsis of each kind of angel and a table for reference to augment our study. With this understanding, we will be able to classify the generic usage of "angels" and determine their appropriate category when reading about them in the Bible.

Remember that our purpose is not to idolize angels, but to produce more effective spiritual warfare by gaining an understanding about working with them.

> *Let no one defraud you of your reward, taking delight in false humility and worship of angels, intruding into those things which he has not seen, vainly puffed up by his fleshly mind, and not holding fast to the Head, from whom all the body, nourished and knit together by joints and ligaments, grows with the increase which is from God.*
> *Colossians 2:18–19 NKJ*

Angels in the Army

Angels Assigned to Heavenly Duty

For the purpose of this study we must consider that at least three heavens exist, namely, the earthly atmosphere, the expanse, or firmament beyond our atmosphere (Genesis 1:6–8), and the heaven of heavens wherein dwells the throne room of God and His hosts. Although it is not within the scope of this book to narrowly define heavenly boundaries, it will serve us well to understand that there are differences between these three heavens, because certain kinds of angels are assigned to different places.

Cherubim are spiritual creatures who abide in the heaven of heavens. They are assigned as sentinels to specific areas. We see them protecting the way to the Tree of Life in Paradise and guarding the Ark of the Covenant. There are sixty-eight usages of cherubim in the Bible. Most of them deal with their golden image above the mercy seat on the Ark of the Covenant. They have wings and also are the protecting escorts for the chariot of the Lord.

As an additional note, Lucifer was an anointed cherub (Ezekiel 28:14), which explains why he could come into the presence of God (Job 1:6; 2:1). Mankind does not normally deal with cherubim since their primary domain is heaven. Therefore, we have no jurisdiction or authority over them.

Seraphim are also angelic creatures assigned to the heaven of heavens. Like the cherubim, they too are appointed as sentinels, but they are also worshippers. Their specific responsibility is to guard the throne of God, but they also testify of His holiness through their

A Taxonomy of Angels

worship. Since their residence is in the heaven of heavens, not on the earth or in the heaven above the earth, we have no authority over them. We see from Isaiah 6:2 that these creatures fly and have six wings.

> *Above it stood the seraphims: each one had six wings; with twain he covered his face, and with twain he covered his feet, and with twain he did fly.*
> Isaiah 6:2

Living creatures are heavenly creatures, too. Like seraphim, Ezekiel saw them in his visitation to heaven. They have the likeness of a man, in that one of their four faces is that of a man (Ezekiel 1:5 and 6). Just as the cherubim and seraphim, they have the responsibility to protect, but their specific assignment is to guard the movement of holy things, rather than the stationary throne of God (Ezekiel 1:19). Ezekiel 10:15 refers to cherubim as living creatures. Although cherubim are living creatures, this specific category of angels called "living creatures" have a different assignment than the cherubim. The point to remember is that mankind does not have a relationship with these living creatures and, therefore, has no authority to marshal them into battle.

Worshipping spirits are those angels who worship before the throne of God. Though not called by this name, their presence and function can be seen throughout the book of Revelation (see Revelation 5:11 and 7:11). Like cherubim, seraphim, and living creatures, worshipping spirits have been seen and recorded by men who have visited heaven. The worshipping spirits were in all likelihood the angelic beings who bore witness to the birth of Jesus in Luke 2:13 and 14. As previously stated, they (like all other heavenly assigned angels) are not primarily assigned to earth but can be given orders to appear on the earth as directed by God. Mankind has only indirect dealings with them and therefore does not interact with them in the army of the Lord. However, this does not mean that they could not be dispatched by God Himself to participate in the battles.

These four classifications of angels are primarily assigned to heaven and have little or no dealings with men. They are under the authority of God the Father and the Lord Jesus Christ, since all authority in heaven and earth has been given to Him (Matthew 28:18 NKJ). If these four kinds of heavenly assigned angels have affairs on earth, the Lord Himself directs them and does not use the voice and authority of mankind.

Angels Assigned to Earthly Duty

There are three categories of angels that God designed to minister to and for men. Two of these are still on active duty, while the other is chained in Tartarus because of disobedience. The two categories presently ministering on the earth and/or within the earth's atmosphere (heaven) are archangels and ministering spirits. The category chained in Tartarus are the beings referred to as watchers.[8] For our purposes, the main emphasis is on archangels and ministering spirits, but to be thorough in our taxonomy, watchers will be explained, also.

Watchers are those angels who were assigned to

earth to watch over mankind and to serve as teachers and instructors. Reference is made to them in Genesis 6:2 and 4 where they were called sons of God. They were apparently given physical bodies in which to dwell and serve, but were corrupted by their lust for women. Because of this lust, they chose to leave their first estate to live on earth as men (Jude 6) and have sexual intercourse with women. The offspring of this union are hybrid beings called *nephilim* (see Genesis 6:4).

Consequently, this kind of angel was responsible for the corruption of mankind and the need for the flood of Noah's time to purify the earth. God punished the watchers for their defection and chained them in Tartarus,[9] where they await God's judgment. Mankind has no dealings with them now. Perhaps they will be the angels that mankind will judge (1 Corinthians 6:3). They are not contributing entities in spiritual warfare because they are chained and, therefore, unable to interact with anyone—man, demon, or other angels.

Archangels are angelic beings assigned to earth and its atmosphere. Their very name indicates that they are the highest rank and order of angels serving (protecting) the earth (*arche* is the Greek word that means "first in order"). This is why they are referred to as princes, which we learn by cross-referencing Jude 9 and Daniel 10:13 and 21. Michael is called an archangel and also a prince—the prince angel of Israel.

When Jesus descends to gather the church, He will be preceded by the voice of an archangel. Comparing this event to the voices of angels in Revelation 8:13; 9:13; 10:7–8; 14:7–9, 13; 16:17; and 19:17, it may be deduced that these are archangels who will serve the Lord in distributing justice and judgment on the earth. This is quite possible since archangels are assigned to earth and have the function of carrying out orders to build the kingdom of God on the earth. If the angels carrying out the orders of the Lord in Revelation are in fact archangels, it may be concluded that these archangels have access to and from heaven to earth and are quite possibly the emissaries from heaven to earth referred to in Revelation 1:4; 3:1; 4:5 and 5:6.

The seven spirits mentioned in the book of Revelation (Revelation 3:1; 4:5; 5:6) may be archangels. This is interesting to note in light of a similar reference in the Book of Enoch, chapter 20, where we find the names of seven chief princes or archangels.[10] These names become more important when we begin studying the releasing of angels into battle from the War Rules. The names of these archangels were written on standards, or banners, that were positioned at the strongholds of the army of Israel in the past (War Rule IX).[11]

Ministering spirits are those assigned to earth. They are the primary servants who carry out spiritual directives in warfare. The word for "ministering" spirits is the Greek word *leitourgos*. It has the connotation of being a public worker or a servant for people. Hebrews 1:14 states that they minister for heirs of salvation.

> But to which of the angels has He ever said: "Sit at My right hand, Till I make Your enemies Your footstool"? Are they not all ministering spirits sent forth to minister for those who will inherit

A Taxonomy of Angels

salvation?

Hebrews 1:13–14 NKJ

Hebrews 1:7 also refers to these angels, calling them a flame of fire. An example of this kind of angel could be the one who ascended into the flame when dealing with Samson's parents in Judges 13:20.

> *So Manoah took the young goat with the grain offering, and offered it upon the rock to the LORD. And He did a wondrous thing while Manoah and his wife looked on: as the flame went up toward heaven from the altar, it happened that the Angel of the LORD ascended in the flame of the altar. When Manoah and his wife saw this, they fell on their faces to the ground. When the Angel of the LORD appeared no more to Manoah and his wife, then Manoah knew that He was the Angel of the LORD.*
>
> *Judges 13:19–21 NKJ*

We may assume that ministering spirits are assigned to people to help them accomplish what the Lord has authorized them to do, according to the anointing of their responsibility. We see them ministering to Daniel, Elijah, and Jesus.[12]

On the following page you will find a chart which details each category of angel, lists its function, and provides corresponding biblical references.

ANGELS IN THE ARMY

**Kinds of Angels   Reference
Function**

Cherubim   Ezekiel 28:14; Job 1:6; 2:1

Assigned to the heaven of heavens. Protect the areas to which they are assigned (Ark of the Covenant, tree of life, etc.). We have no authority over them.

Seraphim   Isaiah 6:2, 6

Assigned to the heaven of heavens. They protect but are also worshippers. They protect the throne of God and testify of His holiness. We have no authority over them.

Living Creatures   Ezekiel 1:5-6, 19

Assigned to the heaven of heavens. They protect the movement of holy things. We have no authority over them.

Worshipping Spirits   Rev. 5:11; 7:11; Luke 2:13–14

Primarily assigned to the heaven of heavens but can appear on earth as directed. They have a function to worship before the throne of God. We have no authority over them.

Watchers   Genesis 6:2, 4; Jude 6

Were assigned to earth. They watched over and instructed mankind. They were corrupted by lust and left their first estate. They are chained in Tartarus, and we have no dealings with them.

Archangels   Daniel 10:13, 21; Jude 9

Assigned to earth and earth's atmosphere. They carry out orders to build the kingdom of God on earth. They have access to and from the heaven of heavens and may serve as emissaries to earth.

Ministering Spirits   Dan. 10:11, 18; 1 Kings 19:7;
                            Matt. 4:11; Mark 1:13; Heb. 1:7, 14

Assigned to earth and the earth's atmosphere. They are the primary servants who carry out spiritual directives in warfare. They are assigned to people to help them accomplish what the Lord has authorized them to do.

A Taxonomy of Angels

Through this taxonomy, we have discovered that there are classes of angels who are assigned to heaven, while others are assigned to earth. So, do we have the authority to command all these angels into battle? No. However, we do have authority to command those categories of angels who are assigned to minister on earth. These mighty warriors spell destruction and mayhem to Satan's kingdom. When we learn how to engage these angelic beings who excel in strength, we will be in a better position to build the church and God's kingdom on the earth.

In the Introduction I made reference to "The War Rules" (see Appendix A). This is relative to our discussion of angels for a basic reason—there is a paragraph summarizing this taxonomy that is breath taking.

(As abundant as the documentation is from the Word of God, the Dead Sea Scrolls give us even more clarion details. From War Rule XII, we can see the kinds of angels and a description of the interaction of men and angels in the Lord's army. The brackets are my insertion.)

> *For the multitude of the Holy Ones is with Thee in heaven [cherubim, seraphim, and living creatures], and the host of the Angels in Thy holy abode [worshipping spirits], praising Thy name. And Thou hast established in a community for Thyself the elect of Thy holy people . . . Thou wilt muster the hosts of Thine elect [men in the army] in their Thousands and Myriads, with Thy Holy Ones and with Thine Angels*

Angels in the Army

[archangels and ministering spirits], that they may be mighty in battle, and may smite the rebels of the earth [the fallen archangel and his angelic hosts] by Thy great judgements and that they [the army of men] may triumph together with the elect of heaven [the angelic host].

I need to make a statement about The War Rules and the entire contribution of the Dead Sea Scrolls. Even though this falls in the middle of the chapter on angel taxonomy, I need to state it now, early in the book, so that proper attention and gravity can be given to this subject.

Around 150 B.C. the Essene scribes were convinced, whether by common sense or by revelation, that the nation of Israel would be destroyed. To preserve spiritual truth and Israel's heritage, they carefully stored various manuscripts in caves along the shore of the Dead Sea. How fortunate we are that they did!

When the armies of Rome plundered the Temple in Jerusalem in A.D. 70, almost all spiritual texts and historical documents were destroyed. When the Dead Sea Scrolls were discovered in 1947, the entire Jewish heritage and spiritual practices were reclaimed.

Knowledge about many things was found—culturally and especially spiritually, from the Dead Sea Scrolls. From the War Rules particularly we can regain vital understanding that the devil tried to bury. Had this information never been lost, perhaps the Christian world would not have had to go through the Dark Ages. Regardless, the recovery of the Dead Sea Scrolls allows us to examine Israel, its culture and spiritual operation of warfare principles, untarnished by intervening history.[13]

Historically, the ancient world trembled when Israel entered a war. Why? Because an unseen army aided them. It is my sincere belief that God had the Dead Sea Scrolls (especially The War Rules) discovered almost simultaneously with Israel's revitalization for fulfillment of prophetic purposes. When we grasp the knowledge of angelic intervention, we might discover what Satan tried to hide by obscuring Israel's strategic and tactical methods of warfare operations (and what God wants recovered through the Dead Sea Scrolls). As you read the next paragraph you will begin to see what I mean. (I have also enclosed the entire War Rules as an appendix to further our understanding.)

In the coming chapters, we will see the commonalities between angels and men and how they interact. We will note the order in the army. Are there angels in the army? Yes. Do we work with them? Yes, but only those whom God has assigned to us. When we learn how this works, we will unleash angels into battle who have been languishing and jobless for millennia. They are well rested, fresh, and waiting for their marching orders. We will see that they are the foot soldiers and that we, as disciples of the Lord, are the officers who receive the orders from our King and relay them to the angels in the army.

The gates of hell *shall not* prevail against the church when we bind the enemy by loosing archangels and ministering spirits against the host of darkness.

ANGELS IN THE ARMY

And when the servant of the man of God arose early and went out, there was an army, surrounding the city with horses and chariots. And his servant said to him, "Alas, my master! What shall we do?"

So he answered, "Do not fear, for those who are with us are more than those who are with them."

And Elisha prayed, and said, "Lord, I pray, open his eyes that he may see." Then the Lord opened the eyes of the young man, and he saw. And behold, the mountain was full of horses and chariots of fire all around Elisha.

2 Kings 6:15-17 NKJ

CHAPTER 2
ANGELS AND MEN IN THE ARMY

In this chapter, we are going to examine the scriptural evidence that angels and men are serving in the army together. As clear as this is from the Bible, additional documentation from the Dead Sea Scrolls is absolutely breathtaking. God wants us to know our fellow members in the army and to fully understand our relationship with them.

There is little doubt that both angels and men are in the army. From the following verses in 2 Chronicles, we see the cause and effect of a man doing something and the resulting response of an angel.

> *Hezekiah the king, and the prophet Isaiah the son of Amoz, prayed and cried to heaven.*[14] *And the LORD sent an angel, which cut off all the mighty men of valour, and the leaders and*

> *captains in the camp of the king of Assyria. So he returned with shame of face to his own land. And when he was come into the house of his god, they that came forth of his own bowels slew him there with the sword.*
> *2 Chronicles 32:20–21 NKJ*

At this point in time, the Assyrian army was considered THE most powerful in the ancient world. If Satan wanted Israel destroyed, he would have to take away their weapons. He accomplished this when he hid "angels in the army."

Evidence showing that men and angels work alongside each other to bring to pass the will of God abounds. We see angels responding to the needs of men and women (Genesis 21:17). "The angel of the Lord encamps all around those who fear Him" (Psalm 34:7 NKJ). Angels ministered to Jesus, Elijah, and Daniel. The church prayed for Peter and the angel of the Lord released him from jail (Acts 12:5–7).

War Rule XII in the Dead Sea Scrolls shows both angels and men in the army. The "Hero of war" is a prophetic profile of our commander-in-chief, the Lord Jesus Christ.

> *Valiant Warriors of the angelic host are among [fighting with] our numbered men, and the Hero of war [the Commander-in-Chief] is with our congregation; the host of His spirits [angels] is with our foot-soldiers [men] and horsemen.*

Angels AND Men in the Army

We have the Bible as well as the Dead Sea Scrolls witnessing of angels AND men in the army of the Lord. We also can see Satan's fear of what will happen when this information is re-discovered. "I hear the sound of the army of the Lord." It includes angels AND men.

Commonalities of Angels and Men

The commonalities of angels and men are something that we often overlook because we tend to focus on their differences. As we examine their likenesses, the contrasts become slight indeed. The differences of our function will be elaborated upon in the following chapter.

Both angels and men are called "sons of God." ("Men" and "sons" are both used generically and are not gender biased. This applies to both men and women, and sons and daughters.) Genesis 2:1 states that "all the host" of the heavens and earth were created by the sixth day. God is the Father (Creator) of both men and angels; they both share the title of "sons of God."

> Genesis 6:2 and 4; Job 1:6; 2:1 and 38:7 refer to angels as the sons of God.

> John 1:12; Romans 8:14,19; Philippians 2:15; 1 John 3:1 and 2 show men as the sons of God.

Both angels and men have free will and the God-given capacity to choose their own destiny. According to 2 Peter 2:4 and Jude 6, some angels, by their own volition, chose to leave their first estate.[15] 2 Peter 2:4 says they are "reserved unto judgment," and Jude 6

Angels in the Army

says they are "reserved in everlasting chains under darkness unto the judgment of the great day."

Both will be judged for their actions.

> 1 Corinthians 6:3 and 2 Peter 2:4 show the judgment of angels.

> 2 Corinthians 5:10 and Revelation 20:11–13 show the judgment of men.

Both angels and men were created to worship God.

> Revelation 7:11—angels

> Philippians 3:3—men

Both angels and men war for the supremacy of God's rulership.

> Revelation 12:7—angels

> Ephesians 6:12—men

Both angels and men are under the authority of Jesus Christ as the commander-in-chief of the Lord's army and are assigned functions within the army.

> Matthew 28:18—heaven (angels) and earth (men)

Both angels and men use words as weapons of warfare.

> Jude 9—angels

> Revelation 12:11—men

This similarity of using words is where we will begin to

Angels AND Men in the Army

see divergence in our functions. Angels respond to the words of men (especially when they pray), coming to their aid when sent by the Lord. Mankind has been positioned within the army to exercise rulership over God's creation through the authoritative use of words (prayers, proclamations, etc.). Angels help.

Without question, both mankind and angels have common qualities and serve together in the army of the Lord. In our next chapter, we will see our express relationship: angels are the warriors who excel in strength and enforce the commandments of God as they are directed by mankind, the duly appointed authorities and officers in the army.

Angels in the Army

God the Father wills it;

Jesus the Word speaks it;

the Holy Spirit brings it to you;

you voice it;

angels carry it out.

CHAPTER 3

ORDER IN THE ARMY

One of the greatest misunderstandings about the subject of spiritual warfare concerns order (rank or chain of command) in the army of the Lord. This truth has been deceptively concealed. It was even hidden by a mistranslation in the Bible. The reality is that mankind excels in authority and angels excel in strength. Men are the officers in the army and angels are the mighty warriors who carry out the orders given to them through the words men and women speak under the unction of the Holy Spirit.

For millennia, mankind has viewed angels as superior beings. Hopefully, the taxonomy of angels given in the last chapter has helped to quell some of this confusion. We see from the Scriptures that angels certainly do excel in strength, but mankind has held angels in higher esteem than they should have because of deception. A cleverly disguised mistranslation has been a stronghold for this deception.

Angels in the Army

> *What is man, that thou art mindful of him? and the son of man, that thou visiteth him? For thou hast made him a little lower than **the angels**, and hast crowned him with glory and honour.*
> *Psalm 8:4–5*

These verses have confused men and women for thousands of years. They do not make sense when the rest of the psalm is read, because it emphasizes the authority of man in rulership over God's creation. The problem lies in the translator's interpretation of the word for "angels" in verse 5. The Hebrew word *elohiym* (God) has been wrongly translated as *angels*. The verse should read:

> *For thou hast made him a little lower than **God**, and hast crowned him with glory and honour.*
> *Psalm 8:5*

It is quite predictable that the sinister hand of Satan lies behind this textual anomaly. The word *elohiym* is used 2,250 times in the Bible. Doesn't it seem a little peculiar that it is translated "angels" only **once** in the King James Version? Maybe it should not seem odd when we remember that the first casualty in any war is truth.

Satan knows that if mankind ever discovers that they are, in fact, greater in authority than angels, people would only be one step away from seeing through his web of deception. Putting this truth together with the fact that Satan is a fallen angel, our deduction would most surely spell his doom.[16] We would then realize that he is under our jurisdiction, as well as the rest of the fallen angels who were cast out of heaven along with him.

> *And what is the exceeding greatness of His power toward us who believe, according to the working of His mighty power which He worked in Christ when He raised Him from the dead and seated Him at His right hand in the heavenly places,* ***far above all principality and power and might and dominion, and every name that is named, not only in this age but also in that which is to come. And He put all things under His feet, and gave Him to be head over all things to the church, which is His body, the fullness of Him who fills all in all.***
>
> Ephesians 1:19–23 NKJ

No wonder he muddied the water with a polluted translation of Psalm 8:5!

Now we can grasp the truth that God wanted us to see. Mankind was made only a little lower than God concerning rulership of the earth. All of Psalm 8 testifies of mankind ruling in his God-ordained authority.

> *O LORD, our Lord, how excellent is thy name in all the earth! Who hast set thy glory above the heavens.*
>
> Psalm 8:1

Angels in the Army

Verse two glistens like a diamond, but it also poses a question. How can a baby have strength? What can they do that thou [God] might still [bind] the enemy?

> *Out of the mouth of babes and sucklings hast thou ordained strength because of thine enemies, that thou mightest still the enemy and the avenger.*
> Psalm 8:2

Out of the mouth of babes and sucklings God ordained strength—not out of the mouth of a macho mega-man, but out of the mouths of small children who would simply open their mouths. If a babe does it, look at the power of praise to still the enemy and wreak havoc on the avenger. Mankind is set as God's under-ruler to quell the enemy's uprising by releasing angels into battle. God is not saying that *only* babies can do this, but that *even* babies can do it.

> *When I consider thy heavens, the work of thy fingers, the moon and the stars, which thou hast ordained; What is man, that thou art mindful of him? and the son of man, that thou visitest him?*
> Psalm 8:3–4

Who is man and why does God visit him? Because man is God's under-ruler and guardian of the world. God made man just a little lower than Himself and crowned him with glory and honor.

> *For you made us only a little lower than God, and you crowned us with glory and honor. You put us in charge of everything you made, giving us author-*

Order in the Army

ity over all things—
Psalm 8:5–6 NLT

All things are under man's feet.

> *Thou madest him to have dominion over the works of thy hands; thou hast put all things under his feet: All sheep and oxen, yea, and the beasts of the field; The fowl of the air, and the fish of the sea, and whatsoever passeth through the paths of the seas.*
> *Psalm 8:6–8*

Verse 9 then contains a rhetorical response.

> *O LORD our Lord, how excellent is thy name in all the earth!*
> *Psalm 8:9*

God's name is excellent in the earth when men praise Him and still the avenger with the strength given even to the words of babes. This is what happens when praise is offered to God and utterance comes out of our mouths.

It is clear that the order in the army is God first and mankind second. Now we will see where the angels fit into the army.

Psalm 103:19–21

These verses of scripture, perhaps more than any others, give a condensed understanding of spiritual authority. They reveal how God, who rules from heaven, gets His will and power to the earth. Through this truth, we begin to see the order of authority in His army and the relationship between angels and men.

> *The LORD hath prepared his throne in the heavens; and his kingdom ruleth over all.*
>
> *Psalm 103:19*

Both the Father and the Son reside in heaven now, yet the kingdom rules over all. We see from verse 22 that their dominion reaches earth.

> *Bless the LORD, all his works in all places of his dominion: bless the LORD, O my soul.*
>
> *Psalm 103:22*

Verses 20 and 21 show us how this happens.

> *Bless the LORD, ye his angels, that excel in strength, that do his commandments, hearkening unto the voice of his word. Bless ye the LORD, all ye his hosts; ye ministers of his, that do his pleasure.*
>
> *Psalm 103:20–21*

God the Father is in heaven and is the prime director of all affairs. By His own choice and counsel, He wills whatever is to come to pass. He then distributes this will to His Son, Who is at His right hand. God's will is verbalized by the Word of God. Jesus, as the Incarnate Word (John 1:14) and the Word of God's power (Hebrews 1:3), distributes God's will to the angels who perform it. How it gets to them is the secret encoded in the next two verses.

Order in the Army

> *Bless the LORD, ye his angels, that excel in strength, that do his commandments, hearkening unto the voice of his word.*
> *Psalm 103:20*

Angels excel in strength. Archangels and ministering spirits are the ones assigned to get work done on the earth. From the verse cited above, it is clear that they do His commandments and heed His word. But the missing piece of information is how angels assigned to earth get the word from God who is in heaven. The next verse shows us the answer.

> *Bless ye the LORD, all ye his hosts; ye ministers of his, that do his pleasure.*
> *Psalm 103:21*

Mankind is the key. Along with the angels, we are in the army (host). What God needs, according to His plan, is what even babes can supply—WORDS! Notice that the angel hearkens to the voice of His Word. In other words, the commandment needs to be given. How does this happen? We, his ministers, voice the commandment as God works in us. We do His good pleasure, according to Philippians 2:13.

> *For it is God which worketh in you both to will and to do of his good pleasure.*
> *Philippians 2:13*

God is at work within us by the Holy Spirit. The Holy Spirit is the created presence of God within Christians and He is given at the time of the new birth (2 Corinthians 1:21-22; Galatians 4:6; 1 John 2:27). The

Angels in the Army

Holy Spirit, the third person of the Godhead, is the liaison between the Father and the Son. Jesus said that the Holy Spirit would speak, not of Himself, but He would speak what He hears.

> *Howbeit when he, the Spirit of truth, is come, he will guide you into all truth: for he shall not speak of himself; but whatsoever he shall hear, that shall he speak: and he will shew you things to come.*
>
> John 16:13

The Holy Spirit works in people to speak the words to which angels will respond.

God needs our voices to dispatch the angels. Why? Because we were created as "rulers" to have dominion on the earth. Angels carry out our words. See why even babes can do this? God can still the avenger (Psalm 8:2) with a single word because it looses an angel to do His will when they hearken to the VOICE of His word.

The process of how God the Father gets His work done on earth is as follows:

God the Father wills it;

Jesus the Word speaks it;

the Holy Spirit brings it to mankind;

mankind voices it;

angels carry it out.

Man is the officer in the army who voices the words given by the Holy Spirit. The words originate with God

Order in the Army

the Father and come down through the divine chain of command.

The order in the army of the Lord is:

> **First—God the Father;**
>
> **Second—Jesus the Word;**
>
> **Third—the Holy Spirit,
> the Liaison from Heaven;**
>
> **Fourth—Mankind,
> God's under-ruler;**
>
> **Fifth—Angels,
> those who excel in strength.**

There are many, many occurrences in the Bible that show angels appearing when men or women pray, but the usage of "pray" often limits our application.

"Pray" is the Greek word *proseuchomai*. We have come to accept that this means "to ask." Not so!

Proseuchomai is composed of a root word with an attached prefix. The root word of *euchomai* means "a vow" (Strong's usage 2171). *Pros* means "to direct something toward." Putting these together, shows that "to pray" means to direct a statement, or a vow, toward something for a specific purpose.

Orders in any army are not requests but commands. These are the orders of the King coming down through the officers. Yes, angels show up when men and women (and even babes) pray, meaning to direct their words toward them. The angels have the strength to do God's word and will and men have the authority to speak God's word and will. Both angels and men are needed in God's army.

This is a noble and honorable usage of men's and women's authority. When the true authority of rulership is realized, men and women can step forward and begin exercising their authority as officers in the army of the Lord.[17]

Now that we know our place in the chain of command, we are ready for the next chapter, "Executing the Word of the Lord."

Executing the Word of the Lord

CHAPTER 4
Executing the Word of the Lord

This chapter covers the crux of the issue—do angels obey the commandments of a man or of a woman? We have learned that only certain types of angels are assigned to minister on earth. Now we will see how they work with men and women to bring to pass God's will and dominion on earth.

In the last chapter, we examined in depth the truths in Psalm 103:19–22. We discovered the axiom: God wills it; Jesus the Word speaks it; the Holy Spirit brings it to mankind; we voice it; angels do it. Now we are going to see more specific details about *the word* that angels obey.

A number of years ago, I was having a discussion with a brother in the Lord about the relationship between angels and men. He said, "If angels obey your word, then have one get you a cup of coffee." His point was well taken. Angels do not just obey any whim or desire of mankind—according to Psalm 103:20, they hearken to the *voice of **His** word*.

The voice of the Lord's word is the key issue regarding whether or not angels obey and carry out the directives of mankind. *We need to understand that the Lord's voice is heard on the earth whenever His authoritative disciples speak for Him, under the direction of the Holy Spirit.*

Look at the obedience of angels to the voice of the Lord Jesus Christ when He was present on earth.

> *Thinkest thou that I cannot now pray to my Father, and he shall presently give me more than twelve legions of angels?*
> *Matthew 26:53*

We know that Jesus, the fullness of the Godhead bodily, is in heaven now with the Father. The Holy Spirit, the presence of the Godhead on earth now, speaks, but not of Himself (John 16:13). What He (the Holy Spirit) hears is what He speaks. After receiving the words from Jesus, He speaks them to mankind. Then, as disciples take heed to those words and proclaim them, the angels are obedient to carry them out. This is just as if the Lord Jesus Christ Himself, the authority of heaven and earth, were present on the earth.

Angels hearken unto the voice of His word, but the voice of the Lord on earth is now uttered by His disciples as they receive their orders from the Holy Spirit.

EXECUTING THE WORD OF THE LORD

Upon Jesus' return to earth, He will again be the fullness of the Godhead bodily and angels will obey His word. The sharp two-edged sword coming out of His mouth is the word that angels will carry out. A single word coming out of His mouth will loose an angel to bind Satan for a thousand years.

> ***And out of his mouth goeth a sharp sword****, that with it he should smite the nations: and he shall rule them with a rod of iron: and he treadeth the winepress of the fierceness and wrath of Almighty God.*
> *Revelation 19:15*

> *And the remnant were slain with **the sword of him** that sat upon the horse, **which sword proceeded out of his mouth**: and all the fowls were filled with their flesh.*
> *Revelation 19:21*

> *And I saw an angel come down from heaven, having the key of the bottomless pit and a great chain in his hand. And he laid hold on the dragon, that old serpent, which is the Devil, and Satan, and **bound him** a thousand years.*
> *Revelation 20:1–2*

The power of these angels is the same now if we will speak the word of the Lord as the Holy Spirit leads us. We can deduce that since Jesus ascended and sent the Holy Spirit, and the Holy Spirit gives us words to speak from Jesus, and we represent Jesus as His voice, we are, in part, representatives of the Godhead bodily upon the earth. What spiritual authorities we truly are!

Joel 2:11 also shows the power of the word of the Lord spoken on the earth. This verse shows Jesus speaking in the future on the Day of the Lord, and also reveals the power we have now as we speak under the unction of the Holy Spirit.

> *And the LORD shall utter his voice before his army [both angels and men]: for his camp is very great: for he [the angel] is strong that executeth his word: for the day of the LORD is great and very terrible; and who can abide it?*
> *Joel 2:11*

Psalm 46:10 has long been a hallmark of understanding for people listening to the voice of the Lord. The context of Psalm 46:10 shows what happens when we hear that still small voice and speak out.

> *The heathen raged, the kingdoms were moved:* **he uttered his voice**, *the earth melted. The LORD of hosts is with us; the God of Jacob is our refuge. Selah. Come, behold the works of the LORD, what desolations he hath made [when His authorities speak it into being] in the earth. He maketh wars to cease unto the end of the earth; he breaketh the bow, and cutteth the spear in sunder; he burneth the chariot in the fire.* **Be still** *[and hear his voice],* **and**

Executing the Word of the Lord

> ***know that I am God:*** *I will be exalted among the heathen, I will be exalted in the earth [when His people speak His word]. The LORD of hosts [the army] is with us; the God of Jacob is our refuge. Selah.*
>
> Psalm 46:6–11

He speaks to us in a still small voice (1 Kings 19:12).

Looking at Psalm 103:19–22 again, we can now grasp the deeper meaning of this powerful revelation.

> *The LORD hath prepared his throne in the heavens [where He and the Son abide]; and his kingdom ruleth over all [the earth]. Bless the LORD, ye his angels, that excel in strength, that do his commandments, hearkening unto the voice of his word. Bless ye the LORD, all ye his hosts; ye ministers of his, that do his pleasure [as the Holy Spirit works in you and you speak the word of the Lord]. Bless the LORD, all his works in all places of his dominion [when they are performed on the earth]: bless the LORD, O my soul.*
>
> Psalm 103:19–22

Jesus said to Peter that the gates of hell would not prevail against the church *if* he released the keys to building the kingdom. As disciples, we must bind and loose by the words of the Holy Spirit coming out of us. However, look at the context of operating the keys of the kingdom that will loose the angels of the Lord. The binding and loosing must be a directive given by revelation, not the whim of man or the desire of the flesh.

> *And Jesus answered and said unto him, Blessed art thou, Simon Barjona: for **flesh and blood hath not revealed it unto thee, but my Father which is in heaven.** And I say also unto thee, That thou art Peter, and upon this rock I will build my church; and the gates of hell shall not prevail against it. And I will give unto thee the keys of the kingdom of heaven: and whatsoever thou shalt bind on earth shall be bound in heaven: and whatsoever thou shalt loose on earth shall be loosed in heaven.*
> *Matthew 16:17–19*

The proper way to operate the keys to the kingdom of heaven is to issue orders under the direction of the Holy Spirit. We must speak by the unction and leading of the Holy Spirit; angels will obey these words and execute the word of the Lord.

So, do angels obey the words of men? The answer is most certainly yes—*when men are speaking under the unction of the Holy Spirit.* Angels *flock* to ride upon the words of authoritative individuals, which is what we are when we are speaking by the Holy Spirit. If we are not speaking under the unction of God, we may pray and angels may still come, but to ensure these angels carry out the will of the Father in heaven, we must strive to be led of the Holy Spirit before we speak.

In the next chapter, we will lift the veil on what Satan has been trying to hide from us—the ultimate weapon in spiritual warfare. This weapon is the direct communication of the Godhead in heaven with angels on the earth. We, as God's authorities on the earth, must speak forth words by the unction of Holy Spirit. The earth will melt and kingdoms will move when the mighty warriors of the spirit realm are released to perform the works of God—initiated by revelation (word of knowledge, word of wisdom and/or discerning of spirits), and followed through with spiritual utterance—either speaking in tongues, interpretation of tongues and/or prophecy.

*For he that speaketh
in an unknown tongue
speaketh not unto men,
but unto God: for no man
understandeth him;
howbeit in the spirit
he speaketh mysteries.*

1 Corinthians 14:2

CHAPTER 5

IF THE TRUMPET MAKES AN UNCERTAIN SOUND, WHO WILL PREPARE FOR BATTLE?

Little did we know that a seemingly insignificant verse of scripture from 1 Corinthians was a direct reference from the Dead Sea Scrolls to loose angels into battle.

> *For if the trumpet give an uncertain sound, who shall prepare himself to the battle?*
>
> 1 Corinthians 14:8

Another good title for this chapter could have been, "Loosing Angels through Diverse Kinds of Tongues," but the same truth is communicated—God gets His will done by angels through you.

ANGELS IN THE ARMY

Earlier in this book, we discovered that certain types of angels have been assigned to earth to carry out the word of God (Chapter 2). We also learned that they obey the voice of the Lord as spoken by His legitimate authorities when they are led by the Holy Spirit (Chapter 4). Now we are going to discover the ultimate weapon in the army of the Lord and how to deploy it in order to release the angels into battle.

The common word that ties this verse of scripture from 1 Corinthians 14:8 to the Dead Sea Scrolls is the usage of the word "trumpet." The blowing of trumpets is how angels were contacted and directed in the Old Testament armies. This information has the potential to change our understanding of spiritual warfare throughout the world.

A quote from the War Rules ties the Dead Sea Scrolls directly into the application and usage of trumpets given in the Bible. War Rule X specifically quotes Numbers 10:9 and reveals the true meaning of how angels were moved. First, Numbers 10:9 shows the use of the trumpet.

> *And if ye go to war in your land against the enemy that oppresseth you, then **ye shall blow an alarm with the trumpets**; and ye shall be remembered before the LORD your God, and ye shall be saved from your enemies.*
>
> *Numbers 10:9*

Now the quote from War Rule X:

> *Our officers [men] shall speak to all those [angels] prepared for battle. They*

Who Will Prepare for Battle?

> shall strengthen by the power of God the freely devoted of heart, and shall make all the fearful of heart withdraw; they [angels] shall fortify all the mighty men of war. They shall recount that which Thou saidst through Moses: "When you go to war in your land against the oppressor who oppresses you, **you shall blow the trumpet**, and you shall be remembered before your God and shall be saved from your enemies."

Blowing the trumpets was the call to war that summoned the angels of God. From War Rules VIII and IX, we see the priests sounding trumpets to call the angels and direct the army.

> ...the Priests shall sound the trumpets of Summons; ...the Priests shall sound a second signal; ...It is according to this Rule that the Priests shall sound the trumpets for the three divisions; ...the Priests shall continue to blow the trumpets of Massacre; ...the Priests shall sound for them the trumpets of Pursuit...

All of these trumpet sounds moved the rank of the army. This reveals what "staying in rank" means in different Old Testament scriptures.[18] Soldiers were trained to move with angels by the sound of trumpets. Notice the additional information in War Rule IX for moving angels—the positioning of towers.

Angels in the Army

> *They shall write on all the shields of the towers: on the first, Michael, on the second, Gabriel, on the third, Sariel, and on the fourth, Raphael.*

The usage of towers is a tremendous revelation. The tower is the fortified high ground. Towers were the strongholds of every army. Towers are the high ground that enable men to shoot down on the enemy. These towers were mobile and were moved by trumpet sounds from the priests in the army of the Lord.

Israel's towers, the army's strongholds, had the names of archangels written upon them. Why? The strength of the army is the angels in the battle. The angels, or towers, were moved by the blowing of trumpets. They were not directed by field radios, but trumpet blasts.

> *Blow ye the trumpet in Zion, and sound an alarm in my holy mountain: let all the inhabitants of the land tremble: for the day of the LORD cometh, for it is nigh at hand.*
>
> Joel 2:1

Suffice it to say, angels and the army of the Lord were directed by the sounding of trumpets. This ties our reference into 1 Corinthians 14:8—the direct contact with angels.

Direct Contact With Angels

The context of 1 Corinthians 14:8 reveals God's will concerning our communication with angels.

Who Will Prepare for Battle?

> *Now, brethren, if I come unto you **speaking with tongues**, what shall I profit you, except I shall speak to you either by revelation, or by knowledge, or by prophesying, or by doctrine? And even things without life giving sound, whether pipe or harp, except they give a distinction in the sounds, how shall it be known what is piped or harped? For if the **trumpet** give an uncertain sound, who shall prepare himself to the battle?*
>
> 1 Corinthians 14:6-8

Previously, we learned that angels hearken unto the voice of the Lord. Now we can begin to see the true effect of speaking in tongues. *Speaking in tongues is speaking by the Spirit of the Lord*—direct communication from God the Father spoken into the spirit realm on earth.

> *For he that speaketh in an unknown tongue speaketh not unto men, but unto God: for no man understandeth him; howbeit in the spirit he speaketh mysteries.*
>
> 1 Corinthians 14:2

These mysteries that are spoken are words from the Father sent through the Holy Spirit to mankind.

> *And they were all filled with the Holy Ghost, and began to speak with other tongues, **as the Spirit gave them utterance**.*
>
> Acts 2:4

Angels in the Army

It is flabbergasting to realize the potential speaking in tongues holds for bringing God's power and dominion to earth; *it can be direct communication with angels.*

> *Though I speak with the tongues of men and of angels...*
> 1 Corinthians 13:1a

Speaking in tongues, as the Holy Spirit gives utterance, is either a tongue of men[19] or a tongue of angels. If the language is not directed for a man to understand, then it is in a language used and understood by angels. This is especially true if it is a diverse kind of tongue.[20]

Speaking in tongues is not given to mankind for the purpose of building the understanding or the intellect. It is direct communication with the spirit realm.

> *For if I pray in an unknown tongue, my spirit prayeth, but my understanding is unfruitful.*
> 1 Corinthians 14:14

Here is one of the great functions and benefits of speaking in tongues: It is direct communication with angels and *can* be orders dispatched from the Father, the Son, and the Holy Spirit, through men or women, to the angels. God wisely designed speaking in tongues to bypass the mind and understanding of man, thus eliminating the possibility of human error.

To command angels in the army, God needs your willingness to release your voice to be used by the Holy Spirit. Your voice will release the angels into battle. Speaking in tongues is our greatest weapon in the

Who Will Prepare for Battle?

spiritual arsenal, because it is a direct communiqué between the will of the Father and the power of angels.

I have written an entire book on the subject of diverse kinds of tongues that reveals the power of this operation. I have said many times that Satan has stood against the truths contained within this book because this knowledge would spell his doom if God's children took it seriously.

It is no accident that since the turn of the twentieth century, the incredible increase of Christianity has directly paralleled the increased understanding and operation of speaking in tongues. No wonder Satan tries to hide this empowering gift of the Holy Spirit from the church. Satan has tried to minimize its importance and discredit tongues ever since its re-emergence in Christianity. Satan knew that the operation of speaking in tongues would spell his doom and arm the church with one of the most strategic weapons ever known to mankind and the spirit realm.

Therefore, we can deduce that speaking in tongues represents to the present day army of the Lord what the sounding of trumpets represented to the Old Testament army. It perfectly fulfills all the requirements from the Bible and the Dead Sea Scrolls.

God the Father wills the directive of war and gives it to Jesus, who has authority in heaven and earth. Jesus the Word speaks it to the Holy Spirit, the Godhead's liaison on earth. The Holy Spirit brings the directive to mankind as He gives the utterance to the assigned officers in the army—the Lord's authorized disciples. These men and women speak in tongues (in this case, the language of angels) as they are led by the Holy

Spirit. Archangels and/or ministering spirits carry out the directive. As the mighty warriors who excel in strength, they perform the exploit as a direct order from God the Father working through Jesus, the Holy Spirit, and mankind to the angels. *It is an army operating through a proper chain of command.*

As the trumpet sounded to coordinate the movement of the army of the Old Testament believers and angels, speaking in tongues moves the army of the New Testament believers and angels today.

The order in the army is followed:

God the Father,

Jesus the Word,

the Holy Spirit,

mankind,

and then angels.

There is a breakdown in the chain of command when men and women don't voice the orders given to them. The situation is similar to a lieutenant not delivering an order to sergeants and foot soldiers. Even though the order came from a major, a captain, or a general— and ultimately from the King—it will not be carried out because the field officer did not have his radio turned on or did not obey.

The trumpet that moves archangels and ministering spirits in the army of the Lord is the yielded and directed voice of mankind under the unction of the Holy Spirit. The trumpet *will not* make an uncertain

Who Will Prepare for Battle?

(or incorrect) sound if the voice is speaking in tongues because the Holy Spirit gives the utterance. Although prophetic words in a known dialect will accomplish the same work, *speaking in tongues is the trumpet that most effectively moves angels in the army because it is direct communication from heaven to angelic warriors who excel in strength.*

*"They will take up serpents;
and if they drink anything deadly,
it will by no means hurt them;
they will lay hands on the sick,
and they will recover."
Mark 16:18 NKJ*

CONCLUSION
TAKE UP SERPENTS AND SUBDUE THE ENEMY

It is a bold new day in the army of the Lord. If we will walk out on this fresh understanding of our function as officers in the army, we can march across the world, subdue the spirit realm, and set the captives free.

It has always been God's will for the church to be His army and to teach the despicable fallen angels the lessons of trifling with an omniscient God.

> *To the intent that now unto the principalities and powers in heavenly places might be known by the church the manifold wisdom of God.*
> *Ephesians 3:10*

Jesus commissioned the church to take up serpents and gave us authority over all the power of the enemy.

Angels in the Army

> *They shall take up serpents [principalities]; and if they drink any deadly thing, it shall not hurt them; they shall lay hands on the sick, and they shall recover.*
>
> *Mark 16:18*

> *Behold, I give unto you power to tread on serpents [principalities] and scorpions [powers], and over all the power of the enemy [demons]: and nothing shall by any means hurt you.*
>
> *Luke 10:19*

The Holy Spirit is carrying out His orders and delivering the word to us—the word that comes through Jesus, and initially from the Father.

> *Howbeit when he, the Spirit of truth, is come, he will guide you into all truth: for he shall not speak of himself; but whatsoever he shall hear, that shall he speak: and he will shew you things to come. He shall glorify me: for he shall receive of mine, and shall shew it unto you. All things that the Father hath are mine: therefore said I, that he shall take of mine, and shall shew it unto you.*
>
> *John 16:13–15*

As officers in the army of the Lord, we have been given the sword of the Spirit—the word that comes out of our mouths.

> *And take the helmet of salvation, and the sword of the Spirit, which is the*

Subdue the Enemy

> *[rhema—spoken] word of God.*
> *Ephesians 6:17*

As we speak the word of the Lord (as officers in the army), the angels are waiting to carry out the order.

So we, "pray with all prayer and supplication in the spirit" (Ephesians 6:18) so that angels will have God's directives to carry out.

> *Are they not all ministering spirits, sent forth to minister for them who shall be heirs of salvation?*
> *Hebrews 1:14*

The angels of the Lord have been waiting for their marching orders for millennia. As the church receives this instruction on how to speak by the Holy Spirit—either by speaking in tongues, interpretation of tongues, and/or by prophecy—we will enable the angels to receive direct communication with headquarters in heaven.

Hell trembles as these words are released upon the archenemies of the Throne. "Vengeance is mine says the Lord; I will repay," and He can and will repay now through the words you speak to angels. The gates of hell are about to be stormed by the mighty warriors of the spirit realm—those who excel in strength. They have the strength to flatten the walls of Jericho and to part the Red Sea. They have already thrown the rebels out of heaven and are waiting to wreak havoc on them, but these angelic warriors must be released by the officers who are in the army now, to defend the honor of the name of Yahweh.

ANGELS IN THE ARMY

Our job is to be obedient in the chain of command as the officers in the army and to give forth the command coming directly from the King. These words come from the Holy Spirit and not from our will or direction. As we yield to the Holy Spirit to speak what He wants spoken, either in tongues or by prophetic declaration, retribution and revenge will be deployed against the rebels.

Demons asked Jesus the question, "Are you come to torment us before our time?" Jesus never answered them, but the truth is *YES!* There is a day coming when the fullness of the wrath of God will be revealed against the disobedient spirits who followed Lucifer. But until then, yes, Jesus came to torment them before their time by giving authority to us, His disciples, to operate the keys to the kingdom of heaven.

By binding and loosing, we will send the angels of God into battle against evil spirits. Now the gates of hell *will not* prevail against the church because we, the officers of the army, will step forward and properly release the mighty warriors who excel in strength.

We have received our training on utilizing the keys of the kingdom. We are yielded and willing to allow the Holy Spirit to speak through us to give the angels the commandments of the Lord. Archangels and ministering spirits will hearken to the voice of the Lord, as we are faithful to speak for Him. *We can and will release the heavenly host into the spiritual battle.*

We say through the Holy Spirit, "Angels in the army—***GO!***" We say, "Let the Angel of the Lord chase them." We say through the spirit, "Hearken unto the voice of His Word."

NOTES

1. Barna Research National Surveys Archives, <u>Angels</u>,, 2000, www.barna.org/cgi-bin/MainArchives.asp (subcategory of Beliefs:Trinity, Satan).

2. Angels are also called "sons of God" (Genesis 6:2,4; Job 1:6; 2:1; 38:7). This shows that they are created beings just as people are created beings.

3. Strong's usage #32. It is used 97 times in the Greek New Testament and is translated in the King James Version as "angel" exclusively.

4. Strong's usage #4397. It is used 212 times in the Hebrew Old Testament and is translated in the King James Version 110 times as *angel;* 98 as *messenger;* and 4 as *ambassador.*

5. The number seven is used by God to communicate completeness. (See E.W. Bullinger, *Numbers in Scripture*.) This reveals the completeness of the phylum of this genus.

6. Colossians 2:18 warns against worshipping angels. We will discover that principalities and powers are fallen angels who have deceived mankind into worshipping them.

7. Watchers are the least known category and will need more in-depth explanation. Watcher is the commonly used term from the books of Enoch and Jubilees, apocryphal books that more clearly define these creatures and their functions.

8. This nomenclature is taken from the books of Enoch and Jubilees and must not be confused with the usage in Daniel 4:13,17 and 23. Being a watcher is a function of all angelic beings who are

assigned to earth to "watch over" God's people. More details on these angels and their offspring are available in "Principalities, Powers and Demons," *Episkopos*, LMCI,. Available to read online at www.LMCI.org/Publications/Articles.

9. 2 Peter 2:4 says that these watchers are chained in Tartarus (hell), a place of confinement where they will be held until the Day of Judgment.

10. Their names are Uriel, Raphael, Raguel, Michael, Saraqael, Gabriel, and Remiel.

11. Geza Vermes, *The Dead Sea Scrolls in English, Revised and Extended Fourth Edition* (New York, NY: Penguin Putnam Inc., 1962), 134, line 15ff.

12. Ministering spirits ministered to Daniel in Daniel 10:11,18; they ministered to Elijah in 1 Kings 19:7; and they ministered to Jesus in Matthew 4:11 and Mark 1:13.

13. Dale M. Sides, "An Apologia on Strategic Level Spiritual Warfare," *Episkopos*, Liberating Ministries for Christ International, Inc., August 2003.

14. Matthew 18:19.

15. The Book of Jubilees infers that the Watchers were tempted by Satan to corrupt the seed of the woman in an attempt to foil the prophecy of the Messiah. This shows another commonality; both angels and mankind are exposed to Satan's lies and temptation.

16. Dale M. Sides, *God Damn Satan* (Bedford, VA: Liberating Ministries for Christ Intl.), chapter 4 "It's A Matter of Authority," shows the proper utilization of a proclamation, not just a prayer. Angels are to be ordered, not asked.

17. Dale M. Sides, *God Damn Satan,* (Bedford, VA: Liberating Ministries for Christ International, Inc., 2000), 83.

18. Numbers 2:16, 24; 1 Chronicles 12:33, 38; and Joel 2:7.

19. This was the function on the Day of Pentecost when men understood the languages that were spoken.

20. Dale M. Sides, *Diverse Kinds of Tongues,* (Bedford, VA: Liberating Ministries for Christ International, Inc., 1999) 19.

APPENDICES

For the sake of parity, balance and further documentation, I have included two appendices for additional study and consideration. The first appendix includes the whole apocryphal text of the War Rules to verify angelic involvement in the army of the Lord; the second is the same documentation of angelic intervention from the Book of Psalms.

Appendices are attachments at the end to provide additional proof and information relevent to a particular subject matter. Both of these will reinforce and conclude the matter—angels are in the army and Christians need to release them to accomplish God's purposes through our authoritative words.

APPENDIX A
THE WAR RULES

I made the decision to include the War Rules within this book in order to more properly release these powerful realities into the body of Christ. The scope and understanding you will gain from these timely excerpts from the Dead Sea Scrolls will help awaken a sleeping giant within and prompt you into spiritual action. Having the whole set of rules rather than footnoting selected portions will greatly enhance your understanding of them, and I hope this will increase your hunger to study these more.

I believe that the discovery of the Dead Sea Scrolls closely parallels the reinstitution of the nation of Israel and therefore has special interest for end time affairs. It is obvious by now that I believe these scrolls hold hidden meanings for the church and Israel to learn in order to face the most crucial battles of history. While editing these for this appendix, one of my staff members commented that she could feel the passion for warfare growing within her.

Angels in the Army

May the Lord teach you spiritual truths as you read these principles for physical warfare, and may the passion for our Lord and the desire to wage war against the defeated foe flourish in you. I pray that the Holy Spirit will likewise teach you special strategies for our end time victory.

The excerpts that have been specifically referenced in *Angels in the Army* are underlined in the appendix. These are taken from *The Dead Sea Scrolls in English*, complete and extended fourth edition, as translated by Geza Vermes, and are used by permission.

APPENDIX A

THE WAR RULE
(1QM)

The contents of the War Rule are as follows:
Proclamation of war against the Kittim (I)
Reorganization of Temple worship (II)
Programme of the forty years' war (II)
The trumpets (III)
The standards (III–IV)
Disposition and weapons of the front formations (V)
Movements of the attacking infantry (VI)
Disposition and movements of the cavalry (VI)
Age of the soldiers (VI–VII)
The camp (VII)
Duties of the Priests and Levites
   (exhortation, trumpet signals) (VII–IX)
Addresses and prayers of the battle liturgy (X–XII)
Prayer recited at the moment of victory (XIII)
Thanksgiving ceremony (XIV)
Battle against the Kittim (XV–XIX)

... This work should not be mistaken for a manual of military warfare pure and simple. It is a theological writing, and the war of which it treats symbolizes the eternal struggle between the spirits of Light and Darkness. The phases of its battle are fixed in advance, its plan established, and its duration predetermined. The opposing forces are equally matched and only by the intervention of 'the mighty hand of God' is the balance between them to be disturbed when he deals an 'everlasting blow' to 'Satan and all the host of his kingdom'.

I *For the M[aster]. The Rule of] War on the unleashing of the attack of the sons of light against the company of the sons of darkness, the army of Satan: against the band of Edom, Moab, and the sons of Ammon, and [against the army of the sons of the East and] the Philistines, and against the bands of the Kittim of Assyria and their allies the ungodly of the Covenant*

The sons of Levi, Judah, and Benjamin, the exiles in the desert, shall battle against them in . . . all their bands when the exiled sons of light return from the Desert of the Peoples to camp in the Desert of Jerusalem; and after the battle they shall go up from there (to Jerusalem?).

[The king] of the Kittim [shall enter] into Egypt, and in his time he shall set out in great wrath to wage war against the kings of the north, that his fury may destroy and cut off the horn of [Israel].

This shall be a time of salvation for the people of God, an age of dominion for all the members of His company, and of everlasting destruction for all the company of Satan. The confusion of the sons of Japheth shall be [great] and Assyria shall fall unsuccoured. The dominion of the Kittim shall come to an end and iniquity shall be vanquished, leaving no remnant; [for the sons] of darkness there shall be no escape. [The sons of righteous]ness shall shine over all the ends of the earth; they shall go on shining until all the seasons of darkness are consumed and, at the season appointed by God, His exalted greatness shall shine eternally to the peace, blessing, glory, joy, and long life of all the sons of light.

On the day when the Kittim fall, there shall be battle and terrible carnage before the God of Israel, for that

Appendix A

shall be the day appointed from ancient times for the battle of destruction of the sons of darkness. At that time, the assembly of gods and the hosts of men shall battle, causing great carnage; on the day of calamity, the sons of light shall battle with the company of darkness amid the shouts of a mighty multitude and the clamour of gods and men to (make manifest) the might of God. And it shall be a time of [great] tribulation for the people which God shall redeem; of all its afflictions none shall be as this, from its sudden beginning until its end in eternal redemption.

On the day of their battle against the Kittim [they shall set out for] carnage. In three lots shall the sons of light brace themselves in battle to strike down iniquity, and in three lots shall Satan's host gird itself to thrust back the company [of God. And when the hearts of the detach]ments of foot-soldiers faint, then shall the might of God fortify [the hearts of the sons of light]. And with the seventh lot, the mighty hand of God shall bring down [the army of Satan, and all] the angels of his kingdom, and all the members [of his company in everlasting destruction] . . .

[. . . The priests, the Levites and the heads of [the tribes] . . . the priests as well as the Levites and the divisions of (4Q464)] **II** the fifty-two heads of family of the congregation.

They shall rank the chief Priests below the High Priest and his vicar. And the twelve chief Priests shall minister at the daily sacrifice before God, whereas the twenty-six leaders of the priestly divisions shall minister in their divisions.

Below them, in perpetual ministry, shall be the chiefs of the Levites to the number of twelve, one for each tribe. The leaders of their divisions shall minister each in his place.

Angels in the Army

Below them shall be the chiefs of the tribes together with the heads of family of the congregation. They shall attend daily at the gates of the Sanctuary, whereas the leaders of their divisions, with their numbered men, shall attend at their appointed times, on new moons and on Sabbaths and on all the days of the year, their age being fifty years and over.

These are the men who shall attend at holocausts and sacrifices to prepare sweet-smelling incense for the good pleasure of God, to atone for all His congregation, and to satisfy themselves perpetually before Him at the table of glory. They shall arrange all these things during the season of the year of Release.

During the remaining thirty-three years of the war, the men of renown, those summoned to the Assembly, together with all the heads of family of the congregation, shall choose for themselves fighting-men for all the lands of the nations. They shall arm for themselves warriors from all the tribes of Israel to enter the army year by year when they are summoned to war. But they shall arm no man for entry into the army during the years of Release, for they are Sabbaths of rest for Israel. In the thirty-five years of service, the war shall be fought during six; the whole congregation shall fight it together.

And during the remaining twenty-nine years the war shall be divided. During the first year they shall fight against Aram-Naha-raim; during the second, against the sons of Lud; during the third, against the remnant of the sons of Aram, against Uz and Hul and Togar and Mesha beyond the Euphrates; during the fourth and fifth, they shall fight against the sons of Arphakshad; during the sixth and seventh, against all the sons of Assyria and Persia and the East as far as

Appendix A

the Great Desert; during the eighth year they shall fight against the sons of Elam; during the ninth, against the sons of Ishmael and Keturah. In the ten years which follow, the war shall be divided against all the sons of Ham according to [their clans and in their ha]bitations; and during the ten years which remain, the war shall be divided against all [the sons of Japheth in] their habitations.

[The Rule for the trumpets of Summons and the trumpe]ts of Alarm according to all their duties
 . . . [the trumpets of Summons shall sound for disposal in] **III** battle formations and to summon the foot-soldiers to advance when the gates of war shall open; and the trumpets of Alarm shall sound for massacre, and for ambush, and for pursuit when the enemy shall be smitten, and for retreat from battle.

On the trumpets calling the congregation they shall write, *The Called of God.*

On the trumpets calling the chiefs they shall write, *The Princes of God.*
On the trumpets of the levites they shall write, *The Army of God.*
On the trumpets of the men of renown and of the heads of family of the congregation gathered in the house of Assembly they shall write, *Summoned by God to the Council of Holiness.*
On the trumpets of the camps they shall write, *The Peace of God in the Camps of His Saints.*
And on the trumpets for breaking camp they shall write, *The mighty Deeds of God shall Crush the Enemy, Putting to Flight all those who Hate Righteousness and bringing Shame on those who Hate Him.*

Angels in the Army

On the trumpets for battle formations they shall write, *Formations of the Divisions of God for the Vengeance of His Wrath on the Sons of Darkness.*

On the trumpets summoning the foot-soldiers to advance towards the enemy formations when the gates of war are opened they shall write, *Reminder of Vengeance in God's Appointed Time.*

On the trumpets of massacre they shall write, *The Mighty Hand of God in War shall Cause all the Ungodly Slain to Fall.*

On the trumpets of ambush they shall write, *The Mysteries of God shall Undo Wickedness.*

On the trumpets of pursuit they shall write, *God has Smitten All the Sons of Darkness; His Fury shall not End until They are Utterly Consumed.*

On the trumpets of retreat, when they retreat from battle to the formation, they shall write, *God has Reassembled.*

On the trumpets of return from battle against the enemy when they journey to the congregation in Jerusalem they shall write, *Rejoicings of God in the Peaceful Return.*

The Rule for the standards of the whole congregation according to their levies

On the great standard at the head of the people they shall write, *The People of God,* together with the names of Israel and Aaron, and the names of the twelve [tribes of Israel] according to the order of their precedence.

On the standards of the camp columns formed by three tribes they shall write,. . . *of God,* together with the name of the leader of the camp . . .

On the standard of the tribe they shall write,

Appendix A

Banner of God, together with the name of the leader of [the tribe and the names of the chiefs of its clans].

[On the standard of the Myriad they shall write,. . . *of God*, together with] the name of the chief of the Myriad and the names of the [leaders of its Thousands].

[On the standard of the Thousand they shall write,. . . *of God*, together with the name of the chief of the Thousand and the names of the leaders of its Hundreds].

[On the standard of Hundred] . . .

IV On the standard of Merari they shall write, *The Votive-Offering of God*, together with the name of the chief of Merari and the names of the leaders of its Thousands.

On the standard of the Thousand they shall write, *The Wrath of God is Kindled against Satan and against the Men of his Company, Leaving no Remnant*, together with the name of the chief of the Thousand and the names of the leaders of its Hundreds.

On the standard of the Hundred they shall write, *From God comes the Might of War against All Sinful Flesh*, together with the name of the chief of the Hundred and the names of the leaders of its Fifties.

On the standard of the Fifty they shall write, *The Stand of the Ungodly is Ended by the Power of God*, together with the name of the chief of the Fifty and the names of the leaders of its Tens.

On the standard of the Ten they shall write, *Praised be God on the Ten-stringed Harp*, together with the name of the chief of the Ten and the names of the nine men under his command.

Angels in the Army

When they march out to battle they shall write on their standards, *Truth of God, Justice of God, Glory of God, Judgement of God,* followed by the whole ordered list of their names.

When they approach for battle they shall write on their standards, *Right Hand of God, Appointed Time of God, Tumult of God, Slain of God,* followed by the whole list of their names.

When they return from battle they shall write on their standards, *Honour of God, Majesty of God, Splendour of God, Glory of God,* together with the whole list of their names.

The Rule for the standards of the congregation
When they set out for battle they shall write, on the first standard *Congregation of God,* on the second standard *Camps of God,* on the third standard *Tribes of God,* on the fourth standard *Clans of God,* on the fifth standard *Divisions of God,* on the sixth standard *Assembly of God,* on the seventh standard *The Called of God,* on the eighth standard *Hosts of God;* and they shall write the list of their names with all their order.

When they approach for battle they shall write on their standards, *War of God, Vengeance of God, Trial of God, Reward of God, Power of God, Retributions of God, Might of God, Extermination of God for all the Nations of Vanity;* and they shall write on them the whole list of their names.

When they return from battle they shall write on their standards, *Salvation of God, Victory of God, Help of God, Support of God, Joy of God, Thanksgivings of God, Praise of God, Peace of God.*

[The measurements of the standards.] The standard of

Appendix A

the whole congregation shall be fourteen cubits long; the standard [of the three tribes,] thirteen cubits long; [the standard of the tribe,] twelve cubits; [the standard of the Myriad], eleven cubits; [the standard of the Thousand, ten cubits; the standard of the Hundred,] nine cubits; [the standard of the Fifty, eight] cubits; the standard of the Ten, s[even cubits] . . .

V And on the sh[ield of] the Prince of all the congregation they shall write his name, together with the names of Israel, Levi and Aaron, and the names of the twelve tribes of Israel according to the order of their precedence, with the names of their twelve chiefs.

The Rule for the ordering of the battle divisions to complete a front formation when their host has reached its full number

The formation shall consist of one thousand men ranked seven lines deep, each man standing behind the other.

They shall all hold shields of bronze burnished like mirrors. The shield shall be edged with an interlaced border and with inlaid ornament, a work of art in pure gold and silver and bronze and precious stones, a many-coloured design worked by a craftsman. The length of the shield shall be two and a half cubits and its width one and a half cubits.

In their hands they shall hold a spear and a sword. The length of the spear shall be seven cubits, of which the socket and spike shall measure half a cubit. The socket shall be edged with three embossed interlaced rings of pure gold and silver and bronze, a work of art. The inlaid ornaments on both edges of the ring shall be bordered with precious stones — patterned bands worked by a craftsman — and (embossed) with ears of corn. Between the rings, the socket shall be embossed with artistry like a pillar. The spike shall be made of brilliant white iron, the work of a craftsman; in its centre, pointing towards the tip, shall be ears of corn in pure gold.

The swords shall be made of pure iron refined by the smelter and blanched to resemble a mirror, the work of a craftsman; on both sides (of their blades) pointing towards the tip, figured ears of corn shall be embossed in pure gold, and they shall have two straight borders on each side. The length of the sword shall be one and a half cubits and its width four fingers. The width of the scabbard shall be four thumbs. There shall be four palms to the scabbard (from the girdle), and it shall be attached (to the girdle) on both sides for a length of five palms (?). The hilt of the sword shall be of pure horn worked by a craftsman, with patterned bands in gold and silver and precious stones . . . *vacat*

When . . . shall stand, the . . . they shall order the seven battle divisions, division after division . . thirty cubits where the me[n of the division] shall stand . . .

VI seven times and shall return to their positions.

And after them, three divisions of foot-soldiers shall advance and shall station themselves between the formations, and the first division shall hurl seven javelins of war towards the enemy formation. On the point of the javelins they shall write, *Shining Javelin of the Power of God;* and on the darts of the second division they shall write, *Bloody Spikes to Bring Down the Slain by the Wrath of God;* and on the javelins of the third division they shall write, *Flaming Blade to Devour the Wicked Struck Down by the Judgement of God.* All these shall hurl their javelins seven times and shall afterwards return to their

Appendix A

positions.

Then two divisions of foot-soldiers shall advance and shall station themselves between the two formations. The first division shall be armed with a spear and a shield, and the second with a shield and a sword, to bring down the slain by the judgement of God, and to bend the enemy formation by the power of God, to pay the reward of their wickedness to all the nations of vanity. And sovereignty shall be to the God of Israel, and He shall accomplish mighty deeds by the saints of his people.

Seven troops of horsemen shall also station themselves to right and to left of the formation; their troops shall stand on this (side) and on that, seven hundred horsemen on one flank and seven hundred horsemen on the other. Two hundred horsemen shall advance with the thousand men of the formation of foot-soldiers; and they shall likewise station themselves on both [flanks] of the camp. Altogether there shall be four thousand six hundred (men), and one thousand cavalrymen with the men of the army formations, fifty to each formation. The horsemen, together with the cavalry of the army, shall number six thousand: five hundred to each tribe.

The horses advancing into battle with the foot-soldiers shall all be stallions; they shall be swift, sensitive of mouth, and sound of wind, and of the required age, trained for war, and accustomed to noise and to every (kind of) sight. Their riders shall be gallant fighting men and skilled horsemen, and their age shall be from thirty to forty-five years. The horsemen of the army shall be from forty to fifty years old. They [and their mounts shall wear breastplates,] helmets, and greaves; they shall carry in their hands bucklers, and a

Angels in the Army

spear [eight cubits] long. [The horsemen advancing with the foot-soldiers shall carry] bows and arrows and javelins of war. They shall all hold themselves prepared . . . of God and to spill the blood of the wicked . . .

VII The men of the army shall be from forty to fifty years old.

The inspectors of the camps shall be from fifty to sixty years old.

The officers shall be from forty to fifty years old.

The despoilers of the slain, the plunderers of booty, the cleansers of the land, the keepers of the baggage, and those who furnish the provisions shall be from twenty-five to thirty years old.

No boy or woman shall enter their camps, from the time they leave Jerusalem and march out to war until they return. No man who is lame, or blind, or crippled, or afflicted with a lasting bodily blemish, or smitten with a bodily impurity, none of these shall march out to war with them. They shall all be freely enlisted for war, perfect in spirit and body and prepared for the Day of Vengeance. And no man shall go down with them on the day of battle who is impure because of his 'fount', <u>for the holy angels shall be with their hosts.</u> And there shall be a space of about two thousand cubits between all their camps for the place serving as a latrine, so that no indecent nakedness may be seen in the surroundings of their camps.

When the battle formations are marshalled facing the enemy, formation facing formation, seven Priests of the sons of Aaron shall advance from the middle gates to the place between the formations. They shall be

Appendix A

clothed in vestments of white cloth of flax, in a fine linen tunic and fine linen breeches; and they shall be girdled with fine cloth of flax embroidered with blue, purple, and scarlet thread, a many-coloured design worked by a craftsman. And on their heads they shall wear mitred turbans. These shall be battle raiment; they shall not take them into the Sanctuary.

The first Priest shall advance before the men of the formation to strengthen their hand for battle, and the six other Priests shall hold in their hands the trumpets of Summons, and the trumpets of the Reminder, and the trumpets of Alarm (for massacre), and the trumpets of Pursuit, and the trumpets of Retreat. And when the Priests advance to the place between the formations, seven Levites shall accompany them bearing in their hands seven rams' horns; and three officers of the Levites shall walk before the Priests and Levites. The Priests shall sound the two trumpets of Sum [mons for the gates of] war to open fifty shields (wide) and the foot-soldiers shall advance, fifty from one gate [and fifty from the other. With them shall advance] the officers of the Levites, and they shall advance with every formation according to all this R[ule].

[The Priests shall sound the trumpets, and two divisions of foot-] soldiers [shall advance] from the gate [and shall] station [themselves] between the two [formations] . . . **VIII** the trumpets shall sound to direct the slingers until they have cast seven times. Afterwards, the Priests shall sound for them the trumpets of Retreat and they shall return to the flank of the first formation to take up their position.

<u>Then the Priests shall sound the trumpets of Summons</u> and three divisions of foot-soldiers shall advance from the gates and shall station themselves

between the formations; the horsemen shall be on their flanks, to right and to left. The Priests shall sound a sustained blast on the trumpets for battle array, and the columns shall move to their (battle) array, each man to his place. And when they have taken up their stand in three arrays, <u>the Priests shall sound a second signal</u>, soft and sustained, for them to advance until they are close to the enemy formation. They shall seize their weapons, and the Priests shall then blow a shrill staccato blast on the six trumpets of Massacre to direct the battle, and the Levites and all the blowers of rams' horns shall sound a mighty alarm to terrify the heart of the enemy, and therewith the javelins shall fly out to bring down the slain. Then the sound of the horns shall cease, but the Priests shall continue to blow a shrill staccato blast on the trumpets to direct the battle until they have thrown seven times against the enemy formation. And then they shall sound a soft, a sustained, and a shrill sound on the trumpets of Retreat.

<u>It is according to this Rule that the Priests shall sound the trumpets for the three divisions.</u> With the first throw, the [Priests] shall sound [on the trumpets] a mighty alarm to direct the ba[ttle until they have thrown seven times. Then] the Priests [shall sound] for them on the trumpets [of Retreat a soft, sustained, and a shrill sound, and they shall return] to their positions in the formation.

[Then the Priests shall blow the trumpets of Summons and the two divisions of foot-soldiers shall advance from the gates] and shall stand [between the formations. And the Priests shall then blow the trumpets of] Massacre, [and the Levites and all the blowers of rams' horns shall sound an alarm, a mighty blast, and therewith] **IX** they shall set about to bring down

Appendix A

the slain with their hands. All the people shall cease their clamour but <u>the Priests shall continue to blow the trumpets of Massacre</u> to direct the battle until the enemy is smitten and put to flight; and the Priests shall blow to direct the battle.

And when they are smitten before them, the Priests shall sound the trumpets of Summons and all the foot-soldiers shall rally to them from the midst of the front formations, and the six divisions, together with the fighting division, shall take up their stations. Altogether, they shall be seven formations: twenty-eight thousand fighting men and six thousand horsemen.

All these shall pursue the enemy to destroy him in an everlasting destruction in the battle of God. <u>The Priests shall sound for them the trumpets of Pursuit,</u> and they shall deploy against all the enemy in a pursuit to destruction; and the horsemen shall thrust them back on the flanks of the battle until they are utterly destroyed.

And as the slain men fall, the Priests shall trumpet from afar; they shall not approach the slain lest they be defiled with unclean blood. For they are holy, and they shall not profane the anointing of their priest-hood with the blood of nations of vanity.

The Rule for changes in battle order to form the position of a squa[re with towers, a concave line with towers, a convex line with towers, a shallow convex line obtained by the advance of the centre, or [by the advance of] both flanks to terrify the enemy

The shields of the towers shall be three cubits long and their spears eight cubits. The tower shall advance from the formation and shall have one hundred shields to each side; in this [manner,] the tower shall be surrounded on three sides by three hundred shields. And it shall also have two gates, [one to the right] and one to the left.

They shall write on all the shields of the towers: on the first, *Michael*, [on the second, *Gabriel*, on the third,] *Sariel*, and on the fourth, *Raphael*. Michael and *Gabriel* [shall stand on the right, and *Sariel* and *Raphael* on the left] . . . they shall set an ambush to . . .

. . . X our camps and to keep us from all that is indecent and evil.

Furthermore, (Moses) taught us, 'Thou art in the midst of us, a mighty God and terrible, causing all our enemies to flee before [us].' He taught our generations in former times saying, 'When you draw near to battle, the Priest shall rise and speak to the people saying, "Hear, O Israel! You draw near to battle this day against your enemies. Do not fear! Do not let your hearts be afraid! Do not be [terrified], and have no fear! For your God goes with you to fight for you against your enemies that He may deliver you"' (Deut. xx, 2–4).

Our officers shall speak to all those prepared for battle. They shall strengthen by the power of God the freely devoted of heart, and shall make all the fearful of heart withdraw; they shall fortify all the mighty men of war. They shall recount that which Thou [saidst] through Moses: 'When you go to war in your land against the oppressor who oppresses you, [you] shall blow the trumpets, and you shall be remembered before your God and shall be saved from your enemies' (Num. X, 9).

Appendix A

O God of Israel, who is like Thee
  in heaven or on earth?
Who accomplishes deeds and mighty works like Thine?
Who is like Thy people Israel
  which Thou hast chosen for Thyself
  from all the peoples of the lands;
the people of the saints of the Covenant,
  instructed in the laws
  and learned in wisdom . . .
who have heard the voice of Majesty
  and have seen the Angels of Holiness,
whose ear has been unstopped,
  and who have heard profound things?

[Thou, O God, hast created] the expanse of the heavens
  and the host of heavenly lights,
the tasks of the spirits
  and the dominion of the Holy Ones,
the treasury of glory
  [and the canopy of the] clouds.
(Thou art Creator of) the earth
  and of the laws dividing it into desert and grass land;
of all that it brings forth
  and of all its fruits [according to their kinds;]
of the circle of the seas
  and of the gathering-place of the rivers
  and of the divisions of the deeps;
of the beasts and birds
  and of the shape of Adam
  and of the gene[rations of] his [seed];
of the confusion of tongues

and of the scattering of the peoples,
of the dwelling in clans
   and of the inheritance of lands;
. . . of the sacred seasons
   and of the cycles of the years
   and of time everlasting.

XI Truly, the battle is Thine! Their bodies are crushed by the might of Thy hand and there is no man to bury them.

Thou didst deliver Goliath of Gath, the mighty warrior, into the hands of David Thy servant, because in place of the sword and in place of the spear he put his trust in Thy great Name; for Thine is the battle. Many times, by Thy great Name, did he triumph over the Philistines. Many times hast Thou also delivered us by the hand of our kings through Thy loving-kindness, and not in accordance with our works by which we have done evil, nor according to our rebellious deeds.

Truly the battle is Thine and the power from Thee! It is not ours. Our strength and the power of our hands accomplish no mighty deeds except by Thy power and by the might of Thy great valour. This Thou hast taught us from ancient times, saying, A *star shall come out of Jacob, and a sceptre shall rise out of Israel. He shall smite the temples of Moab and destroy all the children of Sheth. He shall rule out of Jacob and shall cause the survivors of the city to perish. The enemy shall be his possession and Israel shall accomplish mighty deeds* (Num. xxiv, 17–19).

By the hand of Thine anointed, who discerned Thy testimonies, Thou hast revealed to us the [times] of the battles of Thy hands that Thou mayest glorify Thyself in our enemies by levelling the hordes of

Appendix A

Satan, the seven nations of vanity, by the hand of Thy poor whom Thou hast redeemed [by Thy might] and by the fulness of Thy marvellous power. (Thou hast opened) the door of hope to the melting heart: <u>Thou wilt do to them as Thou didst to Pharaoh, and to the captains of his chariots in the Red Sea.</u> Thou wilt kindle the downcast of spirit and they shall be a flaming torch in the straw to consume ungodliness and never to cease till iniquity is destroyed.

From ancient times Thou hast fore[told the hour] when the might of Thy hand (would be raised) against the Kittim saying, *Assyria shall fall by the sword of no man, the sword of no mere man shall devour him* (Isa. xxxi, 8). For Thou wilt deliver into the hands of the poor the enemies from all the lands, to humble the mighty of the peoples by the hand of those bent to the dust, to bring upon the [head of Thine enemies] the reward of the wicked, and to justify Thy true judgement in the midst of all the sons of men, and to make for Thyself an everlasting Name among the people [whom Thou hast redeemed] . . . of battles to be magnified and sanctified in the eyes of the remnant of the peoples, that they may know . . . when Thou chastisest Gog and all his assembly gathered about him . . .

For Thou wilt fight with them from heaven . . . **XII** <u>For the multitude of the Holy Ones [is with Thee] in heaven, and the host of the Angels is in Thy holy abode, praising Thy Name. And Thou hast established in [a community] for Thyself the elect of Thy holy people.</u> [The list] of the names of all their host is with Thee in the abode of Thy holiness; [the reckoning of the saints] is in Thy glorious dwelling-place. Thou hast recorded for them, with the graving-tool of life, the favours of [Thy] blessings and the Covenant of Thy peace, that Thou mayest reign [over them] for ever and ever and throughout all the eternal ages. <u>Thou wilt muster the [hosts of] Thine [el]ect, in their Thousands and Myriads, with Thy Holy Ones [and with all] Thine Angels, that they may be mighty in battle, [and may smite] the rebels of the earth by Thy great judgements, and that [they may triumph] together with the elect of heaven.</u>

For Thou art [terrible], O God, in the glory of Thy kingdom, and the congregation of Thy Holy Ones is among us for everlasting succour. We will despise kings, we will mock and scorn the mighty; for our Lord is holy, and the King of Glory is with us together with the Holy Ones, <u>Valiant [warriors] of the angelic host are among our numbered men, and the Hero of war is with our congregation; the host of His spirits is with our foot-soldiers and horsemen.</u> [They are as] clouds, as clouds of dew (covering) the earth, as a shower of rain shedding judgement on all that grows on the earth.

> Rise up, O Hero!
>
> Lead off Thy captives, O Glorious One!
> Gather up Thy spoils, O Author of mighty deeds!
> Lay Thy hand on the neck of Thine enemies
>   and Thy feet on the pile of the slain!
> Smite the nations, Thine adversaries,
>   and devour the flesh of the sinner with Thy sword!
> Fill Thy land with glory
>   and Thine inheritance with blessing!
> Let there be a multitude of cattle in Thy fields,
>   and in Thy palaces silver and gold and precious stones!

Appendix A

O Zion, rejoice greatly!
O Jerusalem, show thyself amidst jubilation!
Rejoice, all you cities of Judah;
keep your gates ever open
   that the hosts of the nations
   may be brought in!

Their kings shall serve you
   and all your oppressors shall bow down before you;
   [they shall lick] the dust [of your feet].
Shout for joy, [O daughters of] my people!
Deck yourselves with glorious jewels
   and rule over [the kingdoms of the nations!
Sovereignty shall be to the Lord]
   and everlasting dominion to Israel.
. . .

. . .   **XIII**   (The High Priest) shall come, and his brethren the Priests and the Levites, and all the elders of the army shall be with him; and standing, they shall bless the God of Israel and all His works of truth, and shall execrate Satan there and all the spirits of his company. Speaking, they shall say:

Blessed be the God of Israel for all His holy purpose and for His works of truth! Blessed be all those who [serve] Him in righteousness and who know Him by faith!

Cursed be Satan for his sinful purpose and may he be execrated for his wicked rule! Cursed be all the spirits of his company for their ungodly purpose and may they be execrated for all their service of uncleanness! Truly they are the company of Darkness, but the company of God is one of [eternal] Light.

Angels in the Army

[Thou art] the God of our fathers; we bless Thy Name for ever. We are the people of Thine [inheritance]; Thou didst make a Covenant with our fathers, and wilt establish it with their children throughout eternal ages. And in all Thy glorious testimonies there has been a reminder of Thy mercies among us to succour the remnant, the survivors of Thy Covenant, that they might [recount] Thy works of truth and the judgements of Thy marvellous mighty deeds.

Thou hast created us for Thyself, [O God], that we may be an everlasting people. Thou hast decreed for us a destiny of Light according to Thy truth. And the Prince of Light Thou hast appointed from ancient times to come to our support; [all the sons of righteousness are in his hand], and all the spirits of truth are under his dominion. But Satan, the Angel of Malevolence, Thou hast created for the Pit; his [rule] is in Darkness and his purpose is to bring about wickedness and iniquity. All the spirits of his company, the Angels of Destruction, walk according to the precepts of Darkness; towards them is their [inclination].

But let us, the company of Thy truth, rejoice in Thy mighty hand and be glad for Thy salvation, and exult because of Thy suc[cour and] peace. O God of Israel, who can compare with Thee in might? Thy mighty hand is with the poor. Which angel or prince can compare with Thy [redeeming] succour? [For Thou hast appointed] the day of battle from ancient times . . . [to come to the aid] of truth and to destroy iniquity, to bring Darkness low and to magnify Light . . . to stand for ever, and to destroy all the sons of Darkness . . .

Appendix A

... **XIV** like the fire of His wrath against the idols of Egypt.

And when they have risen from the slain to return to the camp, they shall all sing the Psalm of Return. And in the morning, they shall wash their garments, and shall cleanse themselves of the blood of the bodies of the ungodly. And they shall return to the positions in which they stood in battle formation before the fall of the enemy slain, and there they shall all bless the **God** of Israel. Rejoicing together, they shall praise His Name, and speaking they shall say:

> Blessed be the God of Israel
> > who keeps mercy towards His Covenant,
> > and the appointed times of salvation
> > with the people He has delivered!
>
> He has called them that staggered
> > to [marvellous mighty deeds],
> and has gathered in the assembly of the nations
> > to destruction without any remnant.
> He has lifted up in judgement the fearful of heart
> > and has opened the mouth of the dumb
> > > that they might praise [the mighty] works [of God].
> He has taught war [to the hand] of the feeble
> > and steadied the trembling knee;
> > he has braced the back of the smitten.
> Among the poor in spirit [there is power]
> > over the hard of heart,
> and by the perfect of way
> > all the nations of wickedness have come to an end:
> > > not one of their mighty men stands,

Angels in the Army

but we are the remnant [of Thy people.]
[Blessed be] Thy Name, O God of mercies,
    who hast kept the Covenant with our fathers.
In all our generations Thou hast bestowed
    Thy wonderful favours on the remnant [of Thy people]
    under the dominion of Satan.
During all the mysteries of his Malevolence
    he has not made [us] stray from Thy Covenant;
Thou hast driven his spirits [of destruction]
    far from [us],
Thou hast preserved the soul of Thy redeemed
    [when the men] of his dominion [acted wickedly].
Thou hast raised the fallen by Thy strength,
    but hast cut down the great in height
    [and hast brought down the lofty].
There is no rescue for all their mighty men
    and no refuge for their swift men;
Thou givest to their honoured men a reward of shame,
    all their empty existence [hast Thou turned to nothing].

But we, Thy holy people, will praise Thy Name
    because of the works of Thy truth.
We will exalt Thy splendour because of Thy mighty deeds
    [in all the] seasons and appointed times for ever,
at the coming of day and at nightfall
    and at the departure of evening and morning.
For great [is the design of Thy glory]
    and of Thy wonderful mysteries on high
that [Thou shouldst raise up] dust before Thee

Appendix A

    and lay low the gods.
Rise up, rise up, O God of gods,
    raise Thyself in [might]!
May all the sons of Darkness [scatter before Thee]!
The light of Thy greatness [shall shine forth]
    [on 'go]ds' and men.
[It shall be like a fire bur]ning
    in the dark places of perdition;
it shall burn the sinners in the perdition of hell,
in an eternal blaze
      . . . in all the eternal seasons.

    They shall recite there [all the] war [hy]mns. Afterwards they shall return to [their] cam[ps] . . .

XV For this shall be a time of distress for Israel, [and of the summons] to war against all the nations. There shall be eternal deliverance for the company of God, but destruction for all the nations of wickedness.

    All those [who are ready] for battle shall march out and shall pitch their camp before the king of the Kittim and before all the host of Satan gathered about him for the Day [of Revenge] by the Sword of God.

    Then the High Priest shall rise, with the [Priests], his brethren, and the Levites, and all the men of the army, and he shall recite aloud the Prayer in Time of War [written in the book] of the Rule concerning this time, and also all their Hymns. He shall marshal all the formations there, as is [written in the Book of War], and the priest appointed for the Day of Revenge by the voice of all his brethren shall go forward to strengthen the [hearts of the fighting men]. Speaking, he shall say:

    Be strong and valiant; be warriors! Fear not! Do not

be [confused and do not let your hearts be afraid!] Do not be fearful; fear them not! Do not fall back ... for they are a congregation of wickedness and all their works are in Darkness; they tend towards Darkness. [They make for themselves] a refuge [in falsehood] and their power shall vanish like smoke. All the multitudes of their community ... shall not be found. Damned as they are, all the substance of their wickedness shall quickly fade, like a flower in [the summer-time].

[Be brave and] strong for the battle of God! For this day is [the time of the battle of] God against all the host of Satan, [and of the judgement of] all flesh. The God of Israel lifts His hand in His marvellous [might] against all the spirits of wickedness. [The hosts of] the warrior 'gods' gird themselves for battle, [and the] formations of the Holy Ones [prepare themselves] for the Day [of Revenge] ... **XVI** ... For the God of Israel has called out the sword against all the nations, and He will do mighty deeds by the saints of His people.

And they shall obey all this Rule [on] the [day] when they stand before the camps of the Kittim

The Priests shall afterwards sound for them the trumpets of the Reminder, and the gates of war shall open; the foot-soldiers shall advance and the columns shall station themselves between the formations. The Priests shall sound for them the signal, 'Battle Array', and at the sound of the trumpets the columns [shall deploy] until every man is in his place. The Priests shall then sound a second signal [for them to advance], and when they are within throwing distance of the formation of the Kittim, each man shall seize his weapon of war. Then the six [Priests shall blow on] the

Appendix A

trumpets of Massacre a shrill staccato blast to direct the battle, and the Levites and all the blowers of rams' horns shall sound [a battle alarm], a mighty clamour; and with this clamour they shall begin to bring down the slain from among the Kittim. All the people shall cease their clamour, [but the Priests shall continue to] sound the trumpets of Massacre, and battle shall be fought against the Kittim *(vacat)*. And when Satan girds himself to come to the aid of the sons of darkness, and when the slain among the foot-soldiers begin to fall by the mysteries of God, and when all the men appointed for battle are put to ordeal by them, the Priests shall sound the trumpets of Summons for another formation of the reserve to advance into battle; and they shall take up their stand between the formations. And for those engaged [in battle] they shall sound the 'Retreat'.

Then the High Priest shall draw near, and standing before the formation, he shall strengthen by the power of God their hearts [and hands] in His battle. Speaking he shall say: . . . the slain, for you have heard from ancient times through the mysteries of God . . .

. . . **XVII** He will pay their reward with burning [fire by the hand of] those tested in the crucible. He will sharpen His weapons and will not tire until all the wicked nations are destroyed. Remember the judgement [of Nadab and Ab]ihu, sons of Aaron, by whose judgement God showed Himself holy in the eyes [of Israel. But Eleazar] and Ithamar He confirmed in an everlasting [priestly] Covenant.

Be strong and fear not; [for they tend] towards chaos and confusion, and they lean on that which is not and [shall not be. To the God] of Israel belongs all that is and shall be; [He knows] all the happenings of eternity. This is the day appointed by Him for the defeat and

Angels in the Army

overthrow of the Prince of the kingdom of wickedness, and He will send eternal succour to the company of His redeemed by the might of the princely Angel of the kingdom of Michael. With everlasting light He will enlighten with joy [the children] of Israel; peace and blessing shall be with the company of God. He will raise up the kingdom of Michael in the midst of the gods, and the realm of Israel in the midst of all flesh. Righteousness shall rejoice on high, and all the children of His truth shall jubilate in eternal knowledge.

And you, the sons of His Covenant, be strong in the ordeal of God! His mysteries shall uphold you until He moves His hand for His trials to come to an end.

After these words, the Priests shall sound to marshal them into the divisions of the formation; and at the sound of the trumpets the columns shall deploy until [every man is] in his place. Then the Priests shall sound a second signal on the trumpets for them to advance, and when the [foot-]soldiers approach throwing distance of the formation of the Kittim, every man shall seize his weapon of war. The Priests shall blow the trumpets of Massacre, [and the Levites and all] the blowers of rams' horns shall sound a battle alarm, and the foot-soldiers shall stretch out their hands against the host of the Kittim; [and at the sound of the alarm] they shall begin to bring down the slain. All the people shall cease their clamour, but the Priests shall continue to blow [the trumpets of Massacre and battle shall be fought against the Kittim.]

... and in the third lot ... that the slain may fall [by the mysteries] of God ...

XVIII [In the seventh lot] when the great hand of God is raised in an everlasting blow against Satan and all the hosts of his kingdom, and when Assyria is pursued [amidst the shouts of Angels] and the

Appendix A

clamour of the Holy Ones, the sons of Japheth shall fall to rise no more. The Kittim shall be crushed without [remnant, and no man shall be saved from among them].

[At that time, on the day] when the hand of the God of Israel is raised against all the multitude of Satan, the Priests shall blow [the six trumpets] of the Reminder and all the battle formations shall rally to them and shall divide against all the [camps of the] Kittim to destroy them utterly. [And as] the sun speeds to its setting on that day, the High Priest shall stand, together [with the Levites] who are with him and the [tribal] chiefs [and the elders] of the army, and they shall bless the God of Israel there. Speaking they shall say:

Blessed be Thy Name, O God [of gods], for Thou hast worked great marvels [with Thy people]! Thou hast kept Thy Covenant with us from of old, and hast opened to us the gates of salvation many times. For the [sake of Thy Covenant Thou hast removed our misery, in accordance with] Thy [goodness] towards us. Thou hast acted for the sake of Thy Name, O God of righteousness ... [Thou hast worked a marvellous] miracle [for us], and from ancient times there never was anything like it. For Thou didst know the time appointed for us and it has appeared [before us] this day ... [Thou hast shown] us [Thy merciful hand] in everlasting redemption by causing [the dominion of] the enemy to fall back for ever. (Thou hast shown us) Thy mighty hand in [a stroke of destruction in the war against all] our enemies.

And now the day speeds us to the pursuit of their multitude ... Thou hast delivered up the hearts of the brave so that they stand no more.

For Thine is the power, and the battle is in Thy

hands!... **XIX** For our Sovereign is holy and the King of Glory is with us; the [host of his spirits is with our foot-soldiers and horsemen. They are as clouds, as clouds of dew] covering the earth, and as a shower of rain shedding righteousness on [all that grows there].

> [Rise up, O Hero!
> Lead off Thy captives, O Glorious One!
> Gather up] Thy spoils, O Author of mighty deeds!
> Lay Thy hand on the neck of Thine enemies
>   and Thy feet [on the pile of the slain!
> Smite the nations, Thine adversaries],
>   and devour flesh with Thy sword!
> Fill Thy land with glory
>   and Thine inheritance with blessing!
> [Let there be a multitude of cattle in Thy fields,
>   and in] Thy palaces
>   [silver and gold and precious stones]!
> O Zion, rejoice greatly!
>   Rejoice all you cities of Judah!
> [Keep your gates ever open
>   that the] hosts of the nations
>   [may be brought in]!
> Their kings shall serve you
>   and all your oppressors shall bow down before you;
>   [they shall lick the dust of your feet.
> Shout for joy, O daughters of] my people!
> Deck yourselves with glorious jewels
>   [and rule over the kingdom of the nations!
> Sovereignty shall be to the Lord]
>   and everlasting dominion to Israel.

Then they shall gather in the camp that night to rest until the morning. And in the morning [they shall go

Appendix A

to the place where the formation stood before the] warriors of the Kittim fell, and the multitudes of Assyria, and the hosts of all the nations [assembled] (to discover whether) the multitude of the stricken are dead (with none to bury them), those who fell there under the Sword of God. And the High Priest shall draw near, [with his vicar, and the chief Priests and the Levites] with the Prince of the battle, and all the chiefs of the formations and their numbered men; [they shall return to the positions which they held before the] slain [began to fall] from among the Kittim, and there they shall praise the God [of Israel]
. . .

APPENDIX B

LET THE ANGEL OF THE LORD CHASE THEM

Perhaps one of the more commonly well known verses of scripture dealing with angelic interaction with men is Psalms 35:5. Who else would God have chosen to make this statement but the warrior's warrior, King David.

> *Let them be as chaff before the wind: and* **let the angel of the LORD chase them**.
> *Psalms 35:5*

Although well accepted for its documentation of angelic intervention, there is a hidden truth in the grammar of this statement that reveals greater insight into the relationship between the commands of men and obedience of angels. It is the usage of the word "let."

To my knowledge little if any work has ever been done on the word "let." What a disservice to God in that this is the first word ever recorded (in English translations) when He said. "**Let** there be light." Other great statements containing this little three letter word have definitely impacted the kingdoms of men and of God, such as, "**Let** my people go," and "**let** not your hearts be troubled."

This little word communicates a big truth in grammar as well as in the text of the Bible. The full explanation takes a little time and thought, but in the end, the revelation it yields will surely shed light on our interaction with angels, as well as the whole truth this word is meant to generate.

"Let" is the common translation of a third person, imperative mood verb. There is usually not a corresponding Greek or Hebrew word found in the ancient texts for it, but "let" must be supplied in English to communicate the third person of the imperative mood. The form of the verb itself expresses the imperative mood, either through a suffix or prefix added to the root stem. (I told you this was going to take some thought and time, so settle in and enjoy the appendix.)

Our knowledge of the imperative mood is usually limited to the second person. This is the grammatical usage of an understood subject (you) with a command directive being given by the verb. Examples of this are abundant. (You) Shut the door. (You) Run! (You) Hang up the phone!

The second person of the imperative mood is a more commonly known usage and is taught extensively in English classes around the world. We know that it communicates a command, but when we get to the third person imperative, this also deserves studying and understanding, because it likewise is quite frequently used in biblical languages.

Appendix B

The third person imperative implies the ability to do, and also permission being granted for an action to be taken. It is an authoritative statement, but the emphasis is on the implied ability to perform the act, and also on the authority to grant the permission for it to happen. Let some examples educate us and then we can examine the hidden truth of Psalms 35:5. (Notice that I just used this when I said "**Let** some examples educate us . . . ")

In Genesis 1:3 when God said, "**Let** there be light," He obviously had the power and potential to release light into His desired energy form. He did not have to make it, but instead, all He had to do was release it because the power already existed. Next, God obviously had the permission to make it happen. In other words, it was not a command in the second person, but an authoritative statement to the created elements (as third person entities), releasing permission for something to happen.

In Exodus 5:1 when Moses said to Pharoah, "**Let** my people go . . ." it also was a third person imperative mood. This implied that Pharoah had the ability to release the people and also that he was to exercise his permission for them to leave. You can certainly "feel" the authority in the statement, but grammatically, it is not a command, but a statement of permission implying the ability was present.

Another example of this grammatical construction is found when Paul said in 1 Corinthians 16:22, "**Let** him be accursed." This is extremely interesting and the scope of this usage is fully documented in my other spiritual warfare book, *God Damn Satan*. This verse reveals that Paul had the ability to curse them and he released it by permission when people did not love (*phileo*) the Lord Jesus.

Similarly, in the usage of "**let** not your heart be troubled" (John 14:1 and 27), the ability "to not let it" was latent within them; not in the ability of God, but within their own ability. In other words, this is not a prayer but a proclamation of authority over one's own self.

In Psalms 35:5, the truth will reverberate in our souls when we see what the verse REALLY says. First of all, this is a warring Psalm and the whole chapter is filled with warfare analogies. This is not a "nice" prayer to save the heathen, but to vindicate wrath upon them. When the verse says to "let the angel of the Lord chase them," it was an authoritative decree being released and not a prayer being offered.

The imperative mood does not imply a request or a petition, but is an authoritative decree to release something within the power of someone to do so. Rather than a direct command in the second person, Psalm 35:4-9 contain indirect commands in the third person. The ability to perform the act was contained in God, but the authority and permission to release it was in David.

Furthermore, these verses have two separate authoritative decrees loosed by David to be performed by angels. The angels were to chase them and they were also to persecute them (Psalm 35:6). The first action was compelling the heathen and troublesome people to be blown about as chaff in the wind, meaning that they were to be blown away and removed from their

Appendix B

sphere of influence by the angel of the Lord. This is a non-aggressive decree, in that they were to be rendered of none effect. The other usage in verse 6 is a very demonstrative decree and a proclamation made for the angel of the Lord to actively persecute them and to do them harm.

There are quite a few warring Psalms which unleash God's wrath by the decrees of authorized individuals. The examples of "let" that we have seen show us that although the ability to perform the decree is not always contained within the individual making the statement, the permission or authority to release it always is.

So, what does this lesson on grammar and the third person of the imperative mood tell us? Permission to loose angels belonged to David and it belongs to all warriors intent upon building the kingdom of God. It is an idealistic improbability that good can be accomplished when evil is present, so the evil must be removed. David released the angels to remove the evil source and to vindicate punishment on the wicked perpetrators.

It is within our authority as disciples and those who are "about the Father's business" to loose angels to do the will of God. "Let the angel of the Lord chase them and let the angel of the Lord persecute them" are authoritative decrees made by duly authorized people. The third person imperative mood gives the permission to loose what God avails. God has the power. He sovereignly wills it. We have the authority to represent Him and to loose the angels to do what He desires to accomplish upon the earth.

Angels in the Army

Angels excel in strength, do his commandments and hearken to the voice of His word. That voice is yours if you yield it to speak the word of God, whether in the second or third person imperative mood. Either command it, or release it to be done. Either way, the mouthpiece that voices the decree is the needed entity to fulfill the will of God and bring it to pass on the earth.

Scripture Index

Genesis
1:3, 97, 99
1:6-8, 10
1:28, 6
2:1, 23
6:2, 13, 16, 23
6:4, 13, 16, 23
21:17, 22

Exodus
5:1, 98, 99

Numbers
10:9, 46

Judges
13:19-21, 15

1 Kings
19:7, 16
19:12, 41

2 Chronicles
32:20-21, 21-22

Job
1:6, 10, 16, 23
2:1, 10, 16, 23
38:7, 23

Psalms
8:1, 29
8:2, 30, 34
8:3-4, 30
8:4-5, 28
8:5, 28, 29
8:5-6, 30
8:6-8, 31

Angels in the Army

Psalms (Contd.)
8:9, 31
34:7, 6, 22
35:4-9, 100
35:5, 97. 99, 100
35:6, 100
46:6-11, 40-41
103:19, 32
103:19-22, 37, 41
103:20, v, 2, 38
103:21, v
103:20-21, 32, 33
103:22, 30

Isaiah
6:2, 11, 16
6:6, 16

Ezekiel
1:5-6, 11, 16
1:19, 11, 16
28:14, 10, 16

Daniel
10:11, 16
10:13, 13, 16
10:18, 16
10:21, 13, 16

Joel
2:1, 48
2:11, 40

Matthew
4:11, 16
16:17-19, 42
16:18, 2
16:19, 2, 3
26:53, 38
28:18, 12, 24
28:19, 3
28:20, 3

Mark
1:13, 16
16:18, 56

Luke
2:13-14, 12, 16
10:19, 6, 56

John
1:12, 23
1:14, 32
14:1, 98, 100
14:27, 98, 100
16:13, 34, 38
16:13-15, 56

Acts
2:4, 49
12:5-7, 22

Scripture Index

Romans
8:14, 23
8:19, 23

1 Corinthians
6:3, 13
13:1, 45, 50
14:2, 49
14:6-8, 49
14:8, 45, 46, 48
14:14, 50
16:22, 99

2 Corinthians
1:21-22, 33
5:10, 24

Galatians
4:6, 33

Ephesians
1:19-23, 29
3:10, 3, 55
6:12, 24
6:17, 56-57

Philippians
2:13, 33
2:15, 23
3:3, 24

Colossians
2:18-19, 9

Hebrews
1:3, 32
1:7, 16
1:13, 15
1:14, 15, 16, 57

2 Peter
2:4, 23

1 John
2:27, 33
3:1, 23
3:2, 23

Jude
6, 13, 16, 23
9, 13, 24

Revelation
1:4, 14
3:1, 14
4:5, 14
5:6, 14
5:11, 11, 16
7:11, 11, 16, 24
8:13, 13
9:13, 13
10:7-8, 14
12:7, 24

Angels in the Army

Revelation (Contd.)

12:11,   24
14:7-9,   14
14:13,   14
16:17,   14
19:15,   4, 39
19:17,   14
19:21,   39
20:1-2,   4, 39

Contact Dr. Dale Sides at:
Liberating Publications, Inc.
P.O. Box 974, Bedford, VA 24523-0974
(540) 586-2622 phone ❖ (540) 586-9372 fax

Please go online and check out our web site at
Liberatingpublications.com.

If you enjoyed *Angels in the Army*, be sure
to read its companion volume,
God Damn Satan.

As Christians, we have been born into warfare,
we might as well get *good* at it!